D0832752

Everyman, I will go with thee, and be thy guide,
In thy most need to go by thy side.

EVERYMAN'S LIBRARY

EDITED BY ERNEST RHYS

No. 981

POETRY

POEMS OF OUR TIME: 1900–1942

When the world is full of trouble,
And is restless in its sleep.

W. B. YEATS

POEMS OF OUR TIME
1900—1942

Chosen by
Richard Church and M. M. Bozman

LONDON: J. M. DENT & SONS, LTD.

Made in Great Britain
by Hazell, Watson & Viney Ltd.
London and Aylesbury
for
J. M. Dent & Sons Ltd.
Aldine House, Bedford St., London

First published 1945

This book is produced in complete conformity with the authorized economy standards

FOREWORD

THE poems in this book are the voice of the English people during the first half, or almost the first half, of the twentieth century. They are the purest expression of the joys, miseries, love, horror, courage, and despair which have swept over us, as the weather sweeps over our island, during a time when history has been a tale of storm and uprooted institutions. War, revolution, social and moral upheavals, new comforts and new embarrassments, all these experiences have contributed to our growth; and as they have affected us singly, as identifiable men and women, the more articulate of us have been driven to the antidote of song. And song, like prayer, is a mirror of experience. Wisdom, and the skill of practice, know how to curve that mirror so that what it reflects is concentrated and diminished to an exquisite proportion and set as it were in a frame.

The aim of the anthologist is to continue that wisdom and that skill by redistilling what the poets have already distilled, so that he may present to the reader, or the browser, an intense reduction of daily life; a poetry of poetry. If, in the present book, this reduction has been rightly done, then here is a concentrated history of our time, an inspired equation of events, upon which the reader may ponder without confusion, or the distraction of fashions, feuds, or the smoke of battle.

Such has been the aim of the anthologists here. We have therefore not been content merely to accept the accidents of chronology and to rank the poets according to their birthdays. That method has no meaning, and is a waste of the significances of the time-spirit. For time is an artist and a critic too. Time loves to make a pattern of the universe and of the fate of men. Why not, therefore, seek time's aid in such a purpose as the undertaking of this book? The forty years of human affairs over which we range surely mean something in themselves, and have played what might be called an exterior part, an overall authority, in our comings and goings. Maybe they are the only observer of our human traffic as a whole.

In this belief we have tried to follow that detached observation, and in our two years' task to collect the poems and then leisurely to arrange them so that their own vitality and beauty are enhanced by what they take from and give to each other. In the course of this work we found that the forty years, at least from the æsthetic point of view, roughly divided themselves into four waves, and we have accordingly so divided the book. Each of those waves has an organic unity, moving through an emotional pattern so markedly that it has drawn the whole gamut of events into an almost-meaningful shape. And after the event comes the commentary or song.

It would not be modest to push the matter further. The reader's secondary pleasure, after the instant delight from any one poem, will be to trace his own recognition of a pattern or tendency in the course of the four parts of this book, and to add to the pleasure of the music a satisfaction in the historical basis. The wedding of these two experiences makes for wisdom and a full humanity.

It may be, too, that the poets represented here will benefit by our method. Each of them, instead of having his work lumped at the beginning, the middle, or the end of the collection, is shown as a living and developing creature of the century, an integral part of it, and according to his capacity a voice of it, strengthening his music as the years feed him. Thus the Yeats whom we glimpse at the beginning, in the first period of the book, is a less fully developed poet than the Yeats whom we discover in the last period. Wars, disillusionments, horrible treacheries, have burned away much of the decoration which he had thought was essential to his muse, and his final music remains a superb but sparse enigma. With others of comparable stature, he moves through the book instead of remaining static, and his gait and gesture—as with all the rest—give the procession a significant variety.

Further, the time-spirit, conjured in this way, becomes already more than latent as a critic of the poets whom it carries in its bosom. We see some of promise discarded, and others coaxed, through suffering and other honours, to an achievement which had not been thought possible. We see some continuous and others sporadic. But whatever the character of each, he adds his quota to the ceremony of time, and is absorbed into the whole, to be enjoyed by the reader not only in his absolute right, but as a contributor to this vast shape which we sense, dimly, to be growing around us; the sculpture which will later be known as The Twentieth Century.

RICHARD CHURCH

CONTENTS

INDEX OF AUTHORS

With titles of Poems, and Acknowledgments

Note.—Under the name of each Author will be found the titles of those of his poems which are included in this Anthology, followed by titles of the books in which the poems appear, the names of their Publishers, and specific acknowledgments to all those, whether to Authors, to their representatives or executors, and to Publishers, to whom the Editors' thanks are due for permission to use this material, all of which is copyright. The Editors also take occasion to thank those Authors, Publishers, Literary Agents and others who have given ready help in tracing sources and owners of copyright. In a very few instances the Editors have failed to trace those whose permission for use of certain poems should have been obtained, and to these copyright owners they hereby tender their apologies.

I

1900–1914

THE DARKLING THRUSH
DECEMBER 1900

I leant upon a coppice gate
  When Frost was spectre-gray,
And Winter's dregs made desolate
  The weakening eye of day.
The tangled bine-stems scored the sky
  Like strings from broken lyres,
And all mankind that haunted nigh
  Had sought their household fires.

The land's sharp features seemed to be
  The Century's corpse outleant,
His crypt the cloudy canopy,
  The wind his death lament.
The ancient pulse of germ and birth
  Was shrunken hard and dry,
And every spirit upon earth
  Seemed fervourless as I.

At once a voice burst forth among
  The bleak twigs overhead
In a full-hearted evensong
  Of joy illimited;
An aged thrush, frail, gaunt, and small,
  In blast-beruffled plume,
Had chosen thus to fling his soul
  Upon the growing gloom.

So little cause for carollings
  Of such ecstatic sound
Was written in terrestrial things
  Afar or nigh around,
That I could think there trembled through
  His happy good-night air
Some blessed Hope, whereof he knew
  And I was unaware.

THOMAS HARDY

CITIES AND THRONES AND POWERS

Cities and Thrones and Powers,
   Stand in Time's eye,
Almost as long as flowers,
   Which daily die:
But, as new buds put forth
   To glad new men,
Out of the spent and unconsidered Earth
   The Cities rise again.

This season's Daffodil,
   She never hears
What change, what chance, what chill,
   Cut down last year's:
But with bold countenance,
   And knowledge small,
Esteems her seven days' continuance
   To be perpetual.

So Time that is o'er-kind
   To all that be,
Ordains us e'en as blind,
   As bold as she:
That in our very death,
   And burial sure,
Shadow to shadow, well persuaded, saith,
   'See how our works endure!'

RUDYARD KIPLING

AT A LUNAR ECLIPSE

Thy shadow, Earth, from Pole to Central Sea,
Now steals along upon the Moon's sleek shine
In even monochrome and curving line
Of imperturbable serenity.

How shall I link such sun-cast symmetry
With the torn troubled form I know as thine,
That profile, placid as a brow divine,
With continents of moil and misery?

And can immense Mortality but throw
So small a shade, and Heaven's high human scheme
Be hemmed within the coasts yon arc implies?

Is such the stellar gauge of earthly show,
Nation at war with nation, brains that teem,
Heroes, and women fairer than the skies?

THOMAS HARDY

ALL THAT'S PAST

Very old are the woods;
And the buds that break
Out of the brier's boughs,
When March winds wake,
So old with their beauty are—
Oh, no man knows
Through what wild centuries
Roves back the rose.

Very old are the brooks;
And the rills that rise
Where snow sleeps cold beneath
The azure skies
Sing such a history
Of come and gone,
Their every drop is as wise
As Solomon.

Very old are we men;
Our dreams are tales
Told in dim Eden
By Eve's nightingales;
We wake and whisper awhile,
But, the day gone by,
Silence and sleep like fields
Of amaranth lie.

WALTER DE LA MARE

ATLANTIS

What poets sang in Atlantis? Who can tell
The epics of Atlantis or their names?
The sea hath its own murmurs, and sounds not
The secrets of its silences beneath,
And knows not any cadences enfolded
When the last bubbles of Atlantis broke
Among the quieting of its heaving floor.

O, years and tides and leagues and all their billows
Can alter not man's knowledge of men's hearts—
While trees and rocks and clouds include our being
We know the epics of Atlantis still:
A hero gave himself to lesser men,
Who first misunderstood and murdered him,
And then misunderstood and worshipped him;
A woman was lovely and men fought for her,
Towns burnt for her, and men put men in bondage,
But she put lengthier bondage on them all;
A wanderer toiled among all the isles
That fleck this turning star of shifting sea,
Or lonely purgatories of the mind,
In longing for his home or his lost love.

Poetry is founded on the hearts of men:
Though in Nirvana or the Heavenly courts
The principle of beauty shall persist,
Its body of poetry, as the body of man,
Is but a terrene form, a terrene use,
That swifter being will not loiter with;
And when mankind is dead and the world cold,
Poetry's immortality will pass.

GORDON BOTTOMLEY

EGYPT'S MIGHT IS TUMBLED DOWN

Egypt's might is tumbled down,
Down a-down the deeps of thought;
Greece is fallen and Troy town,
Glorious Rome hath lost her crown,
Venice' pride is nought.

But the dreams their children dreamed,
Fleeting, unsubstantial, vain,
Shadowy as the shadows seemed,
Airy nothing, as they deemed,
These remain.

MARY E. COLERIDGE

A FAERY SONG

We who are old, old and gay,
O so old!
Thousands of years, thousands of years,
If all were told:

Give to these children, new from the world,
Silence and love;
And the long dew-dropping hours of the night,
And the stars above:

Give to these children, new from the world,
Rest far from men.
Is anything better, anything better?
Tell us it then:

Us who are old, old and gay,
O so old!
Thousands of years, thousands of years,
If all were told.

W. B. YEATS

ARABIA

Far are the shades of Arabia,
 Where the Princes ride at noon,
'Mid the verdurous vales and thickets,
 Under the ghost of the moon;
And so dark is that vaulted purple,
 Flowers in the forest rise
And toss into blossom 'gainst the phantom stars
 Pale in the noonday skies.

Sweet is the music of Arabia
 In my heart, when out of dreams
I still in the thin clear mirk of dawn
 Descry her gliding streams;
Hear her strange lutes on the green banks
 Ring loud with the grief and delight
Of the dim-silked, dark-haired Musicians
 In the brooding silence of night.

They haunt me—her lutes and her forests;
 No beauty on earth I see
But shadowed with that dream recalls
 Her loveliness to me:
Still eyes look coldly upon me,
 Cold voices whisper and say—
'He is crazed with the spell of Arabia,
 They have stolen his wits away.'

WALTER DE LA MARE

THE TWO TREES

Beloved, gaze in thine own heart,
The holy tree is growing there;
From joy the holy branches start,
And all the trembling flowers they bear.
The changing colours of its fruit

Have dowered the stars with merry light;
The surety of its hidden root
Has planted quiet in the night;
The shaking of its leafy head
Has given the waves their melody,
And made my lips and music wed,
Murmuring a wizard song for thee.
There, through bewildered branches, go
Winged Loves borne on in gentle strife,
Tossing and tossing to and fro
The flaming circle of our life.
When looking on their shaken hair,
And dreaming how they dance and dart,
Thine eyes grow full of tender care:
Beloved, gaze in thine own heart.

Gaze no more in the bitter glass
The demons, with their subtle guile,
Lift up before us when they pass,
Or only gaze a little while;
For there a fatal image grows,
With broken boughs, and blackened leaves,
And roots half hidden under snows
Driven by a storm that ever grieves.
For all things turn to barrenness
In the dim glass the demons hold,
The glass of outer weariness,
Made when God slept in times of old.
There, through the broken branches, go
The ravens of unresting thought;
Peering and flying to and fro
To see men's souls bartered and bought.
When they are heard upon the wind,
And when they shake their wings; alas!
Thy tender eyes grow all unkind:
Gaze no more in the bitter glass.

W. B. YEATS

THE STREAM'S SONG

Make way, make way,
You thwarting stones ;
Room for my play,
Serious ones.

Do you fear,
O rocks and boulders,
To feel my laughter
On your grave shoulders ?

Do you not know
My joy at length
Will all wear out
Your solemn strength ?

You will not for ever
Cumber my play ;
With joy and a song
I clear my way.

Your faith of rock
Shall yield to me,
And be carried away
By the song of my glee.

Crumble, crumble,
Voiceless things ;
No faith can last
That never sings.

For the last hour
To joy belongs ;
The steadfast perish
But not the songs

Yet for a while
Thwart me, O boulders ;
I need for laughter
Your serious shoulders.

And when my singing
Has razed you quite,
I shall have lost
Half my delight.

LASCELLES ABERCROMBIE

EAGER SPRING

Whirl, snow, on the blackbird's chatter ;
You will not hinder his song to come.
East wind, Sleepless, you cannot scatter
Quince-bud, almond-bud,
Little grape-hyacinth's
Clustering brood,
Nor unfurl the tips of the plum.
No half-born stalk of a lily stops ;
There is sap in the storm-torn bush ;
And, ruffled by gusts in a snow-blurred copse,
' Pity to wait ' sings a thrush.

Love, there are few Springs left for us ;
They go, and the count of them as they go
Makes surer the count that is left for us.
More than the East wind, more than the snow,
I would put back these hours that bring
Buds and bees and are lost ;
I would hold the night and the frost,
To save for us one more Spring.

GORDON BOTTOMLEY

CLOUDS

Down the blue night the unending columns press
  In noiseless tumult, break and wave and flow,
  Now tread the far South, or lift rounds of snow
Up to the white moon's hidden loveliness.
Some pause in their grave wandering, comradeless,
  And turn with profound gesture vague and slow,
  As who would pray good for the world, but know
Their benediction empty as they bless.

They say that the Dead die not, but remain
  Near to the rich heirs of their grief and mirth.
    I think they ride the calm mid-heaven, as these,
In wise majestic melancholy train,
    And watch the moon, and the still-raging seas,
  And men, coming and going on the earth.

RUPERT BROOKE

LOVE LOOKS TO THE FUTURE

We shall live, maybe, till our world turns grey,
  And peace comes on us as our powers grow less,
  And scarce we shall distinguish happiness
From the opprobrious process of decay:
Yet, 'mid the droop and pathos of that day,
  'Mid songs that cease and wings that acquiesce,
  The fading skies shall one last fire confess,
And love in a great sunset burn away.

Or else, perhaps, because we loved so well,
  And found love apt to life, the end will prove
    A consummation rather than a change;
And, tired in the twilight, we shall spell
  Familiar meanings from the text of love,
    And only find the words a little strange.

GERALD GOULD

THE GREETING

What fettle, mate? to me he said
As he went by
With lifted head
And laughing eye,
Where, black against the dawning red,
The pit-heaps cut the sky—
What fettle, mate?

What fettle, mate? to him I said
As he went by
With shrouded head
And darkened eye,
Borne homeward by his marrows, dead
Beneath the noonday sky—
What fettle, mate?

WILFRID GIBSON

THE NIGHT IS FREEZING FAST

The night is freezing fast,
  To-morrow comes December;
    And winterfalls of old
Are with me from the past;
  And chiefly I remember
    How Dick would hate the cold.

Fall, winter, fall; for he,
  Prompt hand and headpiece clever,
    Has woven a winter robe,
And made of earth and sea
  His overcoat for ever,
    And wears the turning globe.

A. E. HOUSMAN

EIGHT O'CLOCK

He stood, and heard the steeple
  Sprinkle the quarters on the morning town.
One, two, three, four, to market-place and people
  It tossed them down.

Strapped, noosed, nighing his hour,
  He stood and counted them and cursed his luck;
And then the clock collected in the tower
  Its strength, and struck.

A. E. HOUSMAN

DRUMMER HODGE

They throw in Drummer Hodge, to rest
  Uncoffined—just as found:
His landmark is a kopje-crest
  That breaks the veldt around:
And foreign constellations west
  Each night above his mound.

Young Hodge the Drummer never knew—
  Fresh from his Wessex home—
The meaning of the broad Karoo,
  The Bush, the dusty lóam,
And why uprose to nightly view
  Strange stars amid the gloam.

Yet portion of that unknown plain
  Will Hodge forever be;
His homely Northern breast and brain
  Grow to some Southern tree,
And strange-eyed constellations reign
  His stars eternally.

THOMAS HARDY

SONG

Lean out of the window,
Goldenhair,
I hear you singing
A merry air.

My book is closed;
I read no more,
Watching the fire dance
On the floor.

I have left my book:
I have left my room:
For I heard you singing
Through the gloom,

Singing and singing
A merry air.
Lean out of the window,
Goldenhair.

JAMES JOYCE

THE GYPSY GIRL

'Come, try your skill, kind gentlemen,
A penny for three tries!'
Some threw and lost, some threw and won
A ten-a-penny prize.

She was a tawny gypsy girl,
A girl of twenty years,
I liked her for the lumps of gold
That jingled from her ears;

I liked the flaring yellow scarf
Bound loose about her throat,
I liked her showy purple gown
And flashy velvet coat.

A man came up, too loose of tongue,
   And said no good to her ;
She did not blush as Saxons do,
   Or turn upon the cur ;

She fawned and whined ' Sweet gentleman,
   A penny for three tries ! '
—But oh, the den of wild things in
   The darkness of her eyes !

RALPH HODGSON

A WOMAN IS A BRANCHY TREE

A woman is a branchy tree
And man a singing wind ;
And from her branches carelessly
He takes what he can find :

Then wind and man go far away,
While winter comes with loneliness ;
With cold, and rain, and slow decay,
On woman and on tree, till they

Droop to the earth again, and be
A withered woman, a withered tree ;
While wind and man woo in the glade
Another tree, another maid.

JAMES STEPHENS

DOWN BY THE SALLEY GARDENS

Down by the salley gardens my love and I did meet ;
She passed the salley gardens with little snow-white feet.
She bid me take love easy, as the leaves grow on the tree ;
But I, being young and foolish, with her would not agree.

In a field by the river my love and I did stand,
And on my leaning shoulder she laid her snow-white hand.
She bid me take life easy, as the grass grows on the weirs ;
But I was young and foolish, and now am full of tears.

W. B. YEATS

A BUD IN THE FROST

Blow on the embers, an' sigh at the sparkles !
My mother she bid me be wise in time.—
Ashes are white an' the red fire darkles ;
I lost the words, but I know the rhyme.

It may be true,
An' it may be true.
'Tis much to me, 'tis little to you !
Oh, look if a boat comes over the water,
An' call on my mother who told her daughter
That ' Love is all crost,—like a bud in the frost.'

Love has undone me, an' why would you wonder !
My mother she bid me be wise in time.—
The waters have met, an' my head has gone under,
But far, far away there are bells that chime
How love is no liar,
Oh, love is no liar.
' That's only a bird singin' there on the briar.
You'd better be lookin' no more at the water,
But give me your hand an' come home, my daughter,
For love is all crost,—like a bud in the frost.'

MOIRA O'NEILL

TAM I' THE KIRK

O Jean, my Jean, when the bell ca's the congregation
Owre valley an' hill wi' the ding frae its iron mou',
When a'body's thochts is set on his ain salvation,
Mine's set on you.

There's a reid rose lies on the Buik o' the Word 'afore ye
That was growin' braw on its bush at the keek o' day,
But the lad that pu'd yon flower i' the mornin's glory,
He canna pray.

He canna pray; but there's nane i' the Kirk will heed him
Whaur he sits sae still his lane at the side o' the wa',
For nane but the reid rose kens what my lassie gie'd him,
It an' us twa!

He canna sing for the sang that his ain he'rt raises,
He canna see for the mist that's afore his een,
And a voice drouns the hale o' the psalms an' the paraphrases,
Cryin' 'Jean, Jean, Jean!'

VIOLET JACOB

THE HEART OF THE WOMAN

O what to me the little room
That was brimmed up with prayer and rest;
He bade me out into the gloom,
And my breast lies upon his breast.

O what to me my mother's care,
The house where I was safe and warm;
The shadowy blossom of my hair
Shall hide us from the bitter storm.

O hiding hair and dewy eyes,
I am no more with life and death,
My heart upon his warm heart lies,
My breath is mixed into his breath.

W. B. YEATS

HARP SONG OF THE DANE WOMEN

What is a woman that you forsake her,
And the hearth-fire and the home-acre,
To go with the old grey Widow-maker?

She has no house to lay a guest in—
But one chill bed for all to rest in,
That the pale suns and the stray bergs nest in.

She has no strong white arms to fold you,
But the ten-times-fingering weed to hold you—
Out on the rocks where the tide has rolled you.

Yet, when the signs of summer thicken,
And the ice breaks, and the birch-buds quicken
Yearly you turn from our side, and sicken—

Sicken again for the shouts and the slaughters.
You steal away to the lapping waters,
And look at your ship in her winter-quarters.

You forget our mirth, and talk at the tables,
The kine in the shed and the horse in the stables—
To pitch her sides and go over her cables.

Then you drive out where the storm-clouds swallow,
And the sound of your oar-blades, falling hollow,
Is all we have left through the months to follow.

Ah, what is Woman that you forsake her,
And the hearth-fire and the home-acre,
To go with the old grey Widow-maker?

RUDYARD KIPLING

ARAB LOVE-SONG

The hunchèd camels of the night
Trouble the bright
And silver waters of the moon.
The Maiden of the Morn will soon
Through Heaven stray and sing,
Star gathering.

Now while the dark about our loves is strewn,
Light of my dark, blood of my heart, O come!
And night will catch her breath up, and be dumb.

Leave thy father, leave thy mother
And thy brother;
Leave the black tents of thy tribe apart!
Am I not thy father and thy brother,
And thy mother?
And thou—what needest with thy tribe's black tents
Who hast the red pavilion of my heart?

FRANCIS THOMPSON

THE COOLIN

Come with me, under my coat,
And we will drink our fill
Of the milk of the white goat,
Or wine if it be thy will.

And we will talk, until
Talk is a trouble, too,
Out on the side of the hill:
And nothing is left to do,

But an eye to look in an eye;
And a hand in a hand to slip;
And a sigh to answer a sigh;
And a lip to find out a lip!

What if the night be black!
Or the air of the mountain chill!

Where the goat lies down in her track,
And all but the fern is still!

Stay with me, under my coat!
And we will drink our fill
Of the milk of the white goat,
Out on the side of the hill!

JAMES STEPHENS

NOCTURN

I walk, I only,
Not I only wake;
Nothing is, this sweet night,
But doth couch and wake
For its love's sake;
Everything, this sweet night,
Couches with its mate.
For whom but for the stealthy-visitant sun
Is the naked moon
Tremulous and elate?
The heaven hath the earth
Its own and all apart;
The hushed pool holdeth
A star to its heart.
You may think the rose sleepeth,
But though she folded is,
The wind doubts her sleeping;
Not all the rose sleeps,
But smiles in her sweet heart
For crafty bliss.
The wind lieth with the rose,
And when he stirs, she stirs in her repose:
The wind hath the rose,
And the rose her kiss.
Ah, mouth of me!
Is it then that this
Seemeth much to thee?—
I wander only.
The rose hath her kiss.

FRANCIS THOMPSON

REFUGE

Twilight, a timid fawn, went glimmering by,
  And Night, the dark-blue hunter, followed fast,
Ceaseless pursuit and flight were in the sky,
  But the long chase had ceased for us at last.

We watched together while the driven fawn
  Hid in the golden thicket of the day.
We, from whose hearts pursuit and flight were gone,
  Knew on the hunter's breast her refuge lay.

Æ.

OUTCAST

Sometimes when alone
At the dark close of day,
Men meet an outlawed majesty
And hurry away.

They come to the lighted house ;
They talk to their dear ;
They crucify the mystery
With words of good cheer.

When love and life are over,
And flight's at an end,
On the outcast majesty
They lean as a friend.

Æ.

THE OLD WOMAN

As a white candle
In a holy place,
So is the beauty
Of an agèd face.

As the spent radiance
Of the winter sun,
So is a woman
With her travail done,

Her brood gone from her,
And her thoughts as still
As the waters
Under a ruined mill.

JOSEPH CAMPBELL

BEAUTIFUL LIE THE DEAD

Beautiful lie the dead ;
Clear comes each feature ;
Satisfied not to be,
Strangely contented.

Like ships, the anchor dropped,
Furled every sail is ;
Mirrored with all their masts
In a deep water.

STEPHEN PHILLIPS

TORMENTED BY THE WORLD

Tormented by the world, the wise man said :
A rock stands in the sea,
And white the anger of water ceaselessly
Thunders upon that stubborn head.
And I heard the noise of the water say
' Not now, not now, but soon enough, ay, soon
Thou shalt be worn away.'
And I perceived the soul within the stone,
And that it answered the corroding tide :
' Do all thou canst : have me in thy power :
Destroy this body while it is thy hour.
Shall I be injured, I undignified,
Who am my soul, and in my soul
Am God ? '—Whereat the whole
Insult of the storming sea
In one confounding cataract replied,
' What else, thou fool, thinkest thou I may be ? '

LASCELLES ABERCROMBIE

THE VIGIL

How long, dear Sleeper, must I wait,
Watching this calm deny thy death,
Ere thou returnest still elate,
Like victor, crowned with parsley wreath,
From some Elysian haven green ?—
Ere 'neath slow-lifting lids are seen
Thy dreamful eyes, which yet behold
Those friends of an heroic mould,
Who pledge thee there, in Hippocrene ?

' Pledge thee ' ? . . . and prize ! Then nevermore
Will they release thee from their home !
And thou, on that rare-fruited shore,
Must needs forget earth's honey comb,
And the joys checkered with distress,

Of friends who did not love thee less,
Yet lack the port of those who dance
On wave-smoothed sands, as in a trance
Buoyant with everlastingness!

Ah, no! this is my dream, not thine;
Void of the soul that shaped it well,
Thy beauty lies, a fragile shell!
It is the past that was divine,
And nursed thy form and spirit fine!
All perishes! those days are fled,
And Memory's art cannot restore
Her fading pictures of the dead,
That come, come faintlier, come no more!

THOMAS STURGE MOORE

BIRTHRIGHT

Lord Rameses of Egypt sighed
  Because a summer evening passed;
And little Ariadne cried
  That summer fancy fell at last
To dust; and young Verona died
  When beauty's hour was overcast.

Theirs was the bitterness we know
  Because the clouds of hawthorn keep
So short a state, and kisses go
  To tombs unfathomably deep,
While Rameses and Romeo
  And little Ariadne sleep.

JOHN DRINKWATER

AN EPITAPH

Here lies a most beautiful lady,
Light of step and heart was she;
I think she was the most beautiful lady
That ever was in the West Country.
But beauty vanishes; beauty passes;
However rare—rare it be;
And when I crumble, who will remember
This lady of the West Country?

WALTER DE LA MARE

A DREAM OF DEATH

I dreamed that one had died in a strange place
Near no accustomed hand;
And they had nailed the boards above her face
The peasants of that land,
And, wondering, planted by her solitude
A cypress and a yew:
I came, and wrote upon a cross of wood
Man had no more to do:
She was more beautiful than thy first love,
This lady by the trees:
And gazed upon the mournful stars above,
And heard the mournful breeze.

W. B. YEATS

THE LISTENERS

'Is there anybody there?' said the Traveller,
  Knocking on the moonlit door;
And his horse in the silence champed the grasses
  Of the forest's ferny floor:
And a bird flew up out of the turret,
  Above the Traveller's head:
And he smote upon the door again a second time;
  'Is there anybody there?' he said.
But no one descended to the Traveller;
  No head from the leaf-fringed sill
Leaned over and looked into his grey eyes,
  Where he stood perplexed and still.
But only a host of phantom listeners
  That dwelt in the lone house then
Stood listening in the quiet of the moonlight
  To that voice from the world of men:
Stood thronging the faint moonbeams on the dark stair,
  That goes down to the empty hall,
Hearkening in an air stirred and shaken
  By the lonely Traveller's call.
And he felt in his heart their strangeness,
  Their stillness answering his cry,
While his horse moved, cropping the dark turf,
  'Neath the starred and leafy sky;
For he suddenly smote on the door, even
  Louder, and lifted his head:—
'Tell them I came, and no one answered,
  That I kept my word!' he said.
Never the least stir made the listeners,
  Though every word he spake
Fell echoing through the shadowiness of the still house
  From the one man left awake;
Ay, they heard his foot upon the stirrup,
  And the sound of iron on stone,
And how the silence surged softly backward,
  When the plunging hoofs were gone.

WALTER DE LA MARE

SONNET XVII

Because my faltering feet may fail to dare
The first descendant of the steps of Hell,
Give me the Word in time that triumphs there.
I too must pass into the misty hollow
Where all our living laughter stops : and hark !
The tiny stuffless voices of the dark
Have called me, called me, till I needs must follow :
Give me the Word and I'll attempt it well.

Say it's the little winking of an eye
Which in that issue is uncurtained quite ;
A little sleep that helps a moment by
Between the thin dawn and the large daylight.
  Ah, tell me more than yet was hoped of men ;
  Swear that's true now, and I'll believe it then.

HILAIRE BELLOC

THE GHOST

Peace in thy hands,
Peace in thine eyes,
Peace on thy brow ;
Flower of a moment in the eternal hour,
Peace with me now.

Not a wave breaks,
Not a bird calls,
My heart, like a sea,
Silent after a storm hath died,
Sleeps within me.

All the night's dews,
All the world's leaves,
All winter's snow
Seem with their quiet to have stilled in life's dream
All sorrowing now.

WALTER DE LA MARE

ON A SLEEPING FRIEND

Lady, when your lovely head
Droops to sink among the Dead,
And the quiet places keep
You that so divinely sleep ;
Then the dead shall blessèd be
With a new solemnity.
For such Beauty, so descending,
Pledges them that Death is ending.
Sleep your fill :—but when you wake
Dawn shall over Lethe break.

HILAIRE BELLOC

NIGHT IS FALLEN

Night is fallen, within, without,
   Come, Love, soon !
I am weary of my doubt.
The golden fire of the Sun is out,
   The silver fire of the Moon.

Love shall be
A child in me
   When they are cinders gray,
With the earth and with the sea,
With the star that shines on thee,
   And the night and day.

MARY E. COLERIDGE

A CRADLE SONG

The angels are stooping
Above your bed ;
They weary of trooping
With the whimpering dead.

God's laughing in heaven
To see you so good ;
The Shining Seven
Are gay with His mood.

I kiss you and kiss you,
My pigeon, my own ;
Ah, how I shall miss you
When you have grown.

W. B. YEATS

NO CHILD

I heard in the night the pigeons
  Stirring within their nest :
The wild pigeon's stir was tender
  Like a child's hand at the breast.

I cried, ' O, stir no more !
  (My breast was touched with tears),
O pigeons, make no stir—
  A childless woman hears.'

PADRAIC COLUM

MATERNITY

One wept whose only child was dead,
    New-born, ten years ago.
'Weep not; he is in bliss,' they said.
    She answered, 'Even so.

'Ten years ago was born in pain
    A child, not now forlorn.
But oh, ten years ago, in vain,
    A mother, a mother was born.'

ALICE MEYNELL

REST

On me to rest, my bird, my bird:
    The swaying branches of my heart
Are blown by every wind toward
    The home whereto their wings depart.

Build not your nest, my bird, on me;
    I know no peace but ever sway:
O lovely bird, be free, be free,
    On the wild music of the day.

But sometimes when your wings would rest,
    And winds are laid on quiet eves:
Come, I will bear you breast to breast,
    And lap you close with loving leaves.

Æ.

TO C.L.M.

In the dark womb where I began
My mother's life made me a man.
Through all the months of human birth
Her beauty fed my common earth.
I cannot see, nor breathe, nor stir,
But through the death of some of her.

Down in the darkness of the grave
She cannot see the life she gave.
For all her love, she cannot tell
Whether I use it ill or well,
Nor knock at dusty doors to find
Her beauty dusty in the mind.

If the grave's gates could be undone,
She would not know her little son,
I am so grown. If we should meet
She would pass by me in the street,
Unless my soul's face let her see
My sense of what she did for me.

What have I done to keep in mind
My debt to her and womankind?
What woman's happier life repays
Her for those months of wretched days?
For all my mouthless body leeched
Ere Birth's releasing hell was reached?

What have I done, or tried, or said
In thanks to that dear woman dead?
Men triumph over women still,
Men trample women's rights at will,
And man's lust roves the world untamed.

. . . . .

O grave, keep shut, lest I be shamed.

JOHN MASEFIELD

JEAN RICHEPIN'S SONG

A poor lad once and a lad so trim,
Fol de rol de raly O!
Fol de rol!
A poor lad once and a lad so trim
Gave his love to her that loved not him.

And, says she, 'Fetch me to-night, you rogue,'
Fol de rol de raly O!
Fol de rol!
And, says she, 'Fetch me to-night, you rogue,
Your mother's heart to feed my dog!'

To his mother's house went that young man,
Fol de rol de raly O!
Fol de rol!
To his mother's house went that young man,
Killed her, and took the heart, and ran.

And as he was running, look you, he fell,
Fol de rol de raly O!
Fol de rol!
And as he was running, look you, he fell,
And the heart rolled on the ground as well.

And the lad, as the heart was a-rolling, heard
(*Fol de rol de raly O!*
Fol de rol!)
And the lad, as the heart was a-rolling, heard
That the heart was speaking, and this was the word;

The heart was a-weeping, and crying so small
(*Fol de rol de raly O!*
Fol de rol!)
The heart was a-weeping, and crying so small,
'*Are you hurt, my child, are you hurt at all?*'

HERBERT TRENCH

THE STOLEN CHILD

Where dips the rocky highland
Of Sleuth Wood in the lake,
There lies a leafy island
Where flapping herons wake
The drowsy water rats ;
There we've hid our faery vats,
Full of berries,
And the reddest stolen cherries.
Come away, O human child !
To the waters and the wild
With a faery, hand in hand,
For the world's more full of weeping than you can understand.

Where the wave of moonlight glosses
The dim gray sands with light,
Far off by furthest Rosses
We foot it all the night,
Weaving olden dances,
Mingling hands and mingling glances
Till the moon has taken flight ;
To and fro we leap
And chase the frothy bubbles,
While the world is full of troubles
And is anxious in its sleep.
Come away, O human child !
To the waters and the wild
With a faery, hand in hand,
For the world's more full of weeping than you can understand.

Where the wandering water gushes
From the hills above Glen-Car,
In pools among the rushes
That scarce could bathe a star,
We seek for slumbering trout
And, whispering in their ears,
Give them unquiet dreams ;
Leaning softly out
From ferns that drop their tears
Over the young streams.

Come away, O human child!
To the waters and the wild
With a faery, hand in hand,
For the world's more full of weeping than you can understand.

Away with us he's going,
The solemn-eyed:
He'll hear no more the lowing
Of the calves on the warm hillside
Or the kettle on the hob
Sing peace into his breast,
Or see the brown mice bob
Round and round the oatmeal-chest.
For he comes, the human child,
To the waters and the wild
With a faery, hand in hand,
From a world more full of weeping than he can understand.

W. B. YEATS

THE HAPPY CHILD

I saw this day sweet flowers grow thick—
But not one like the child did pick.

I heard the pack-hounds in green park—
But no dog like the child heard bark.

I heard this day bird after bird—
But not one like the child has heard.

A hundred butterflies saw I—
But not one like the child saw fly.

I saw the horses roll in grass—
But no horse like the child saw pass.

My world this day has lovely been—
But not like what the child has seen.

W. H. DAVIES

PRE-EXISTENCE

I laid me down upon the shore
   And dreamed a little space;
I heard the great waves break and roar;
   The sun was on my face.

My idle hands and fingers brown
   Played with the pebbles grey;
The waves came up, the waves went down,
   Most thundering and gay.

The pebbles, they were smooth and round
   And warm upon my hands,
Like little people I had found
   Sitting among the sands.

The grains of sand so shining-small
   Soft through my fingers ran;
The sun shone down upon it all,
   And so my dream began:

How all of this had been before;
   How ages far away
I lay on some forgotten shore
   As here I lie to-day.

The waves came shining up the sands,
   As here to-day they shine;
And in my pre-pelasgian hands
   The sand was warm and fine.

I have forgotten whence I came,
   Or what my home might be,—
Or by what strange and savage name
   I called that thundering sea.

I only know the sun shone down
   As still it shines to-day,
And in my fingers long and brown
   The little pebbles lay.

FRANCES CORNFORD

THE OLD SHIPS

I have seen old ships sail like swans asleep
Beyond the village which men still call Tyre,
With leaden age o'er-cargoed, dipping deep
For Famagusta and the hidden sun
That rings black Cyprus with a lake of fire;
And all those ships were certainly so old
Who knows how oft with squat and noisy gun,
Questing brown slaves or Syrian oranges,
The pirate Genoese
Hell-raked them till they rolled
Blood, water, fruit and corpses up the hold.
But now through friendly seas they softly run,
Painted the mid-sea blue or shore-sea green,
Still patterned with the vine and grapes in gold.

But I have seen,
Pointing her shapely shadows from the dawn
And image-tumbled on a rose-swept bay,
A drowsy ship of some yet older day;
And, wonder's breath indrawn,
Thought I—who knows—who knows—but in that same
(Fished up beyond Ææa, patched up new
—Stern painted brighter blue—)
That talkative bald-headed seaman came
(Twelve patient comrades sweating at the oar)
From Troy's doom-crimson shore,
And with great lies about his wooden horse
Set the crew laughing, and forgot his course.

It was so old a ship—who knows, who knows?
—And yet so beautiful, I watched in vain
To see the mast burst open with a rose,
And the whole deck put on its leaves again.

JAMES ELROY FLECKER

THE WAY THROUGH THE WOODS

They shut the road through the woods
Seventy years ago.
Weather and rain have undone it again,
And now you would never know
There was once a road through the woods
Before they planted the trees.
It is underneath the coppice and heath,
And the thin anemones.
Only the keeper sees
That, where the ring-dove broods,
And the badgers roll at ease,
There was once a road through the woods.

Yet, if you enter the woods
Of a summer evening late,
When the night-air cools on the trout-ringed pools
Where the otter whistles his mate,
(They fear not men in the woods,
Because they see so few)
You will hear the beat of a horse's feet,
And the swish of a skirt in the dew,
Steadily cantering through
The misty solitudes,
As though they perfectly knew
The old lost road through the woods . . .
But there is no road through the woods.

RUDYARD KIPLING

UPON ECKINGTON BRIDGE, RIVER AVON

O pastoral heart of England! like a psalm
  Of green days telling with a quiet beat—
O wave into the sunset flowing calm!
  O tired lark descending on the wheat!
Lies it all peace beyond that western fold
  Where now the lingering shepherd sees his star
Rise upon Malvern? Paints an Age of Gold
    Yon cloud with prophecies of linkèd ease—
    Lulling this Land, with hills drawn up like knees,
To drowse beside her implements of war?

Man shall outlast his battles. They have swept
  Avon from Naseby Field to Severn Ham;
And Evesham's dedicated stones have stepp'd
  Down to the dust with Montfort's oriflamme,
Nor the red tear nor the reflected tower
  Abides; but yet these eloquent grooves remain,
Worn in the sandstone parapet hour by hour
    By labouring bargemen where they shifted ropes.
    E'en so shall man turn back from violent hopes
To Adam's cheer, and toil with spade again.

Ay, and his mother Nature, to whose lap
  Like a repentant child at length he hies,
Not in the whirlwind or the thunder-clap
  Proclaims her more tremendous mysteries:
But when in winter's grave, bereft of light,
  With still, small voice divinelier whispering
—Lifting the green head of the aconite,
    Feeding with sap of hope the hazel-shoot—
    She feels God's finger active at the root,
Turns in her sleep, and murmurs of the Spring.

SIR ARTHUR QUILLER-COUCH

A SINGER ASLEEP

(ALGERNON CHARLES SWINBURNE, 1837–1909)

In this fair niche above the unslumbering sea,
That sentrys up and down all night, all day,
From cove to promontory, from ness to bay,
The Fates have fitly bidden that he should be
  Pillowed eternally.

—It was as though a garland of red roses
Had fallen about the hood of some smug nun
When irresponsibly dropped as from the sun,
In fulth of numbers freaked with musical closes,
Upon Victoria's formal middle time
  His leaves of rhythm and rhyme.

O that far morning of a summer day
When, down a terraced street whose pavements lay
Glassing the sunshine into my bent eyes,
I walked and read with a quick glad surprise
  New words, in classic guise,—

The passionate pages of his earlier years,
Fraught with hot sighs, sad laughters, kisses, tears;
Fresh-fluted notes, yet from a minstrel who
Blew them no naïvely, but as one who knew
  Full well why thus he blew.

I still can hear the brabble and the roar
At those thy tunes, O still one, now passed through
That fitful fire of tongues then entered new!
Their power is spent like spindrift on this shore;
  Thine swells yet more and more.

—His singing-mistress verily was no other
Than she the Lesbian, she the music-mother
Of all the tribe that feel in melodies;
Who leapt, love-anguished, from the Leucadian steep
Into the rambling world-encircling deep
  Which hides her where none sees.

And one can hold in thought that nightly here
His phantom may draw down to the water's brim,
And hers come up to meet it, as a dim
Lone shine upon the heaving hydrosphere,
And mariners wonder as they traverse near,
  Unknowing of her and him.

One dreams him sighing to her spectral form:
'O teacher, where lies hid thy burning line;
Where are those songs, O poetess divine
Whose very orts are love incarnadine?'
And her smile back: 'Disciple true and warm
  Sufficient now are thine.' . . .

So here, beneath the waking constellations,
Where the waves peal their everlasting strains,
And their dull subterrene reverberations
Shake him when storms make mountains of their plains—
Him once their peer in sad improvisations,
And deft as wind to cleave their frothy manes—
I leave him, while the daylight gleam declines
  Upon the capes and chines.

THOMAS HARDY

THE SOUTH COUNTRY

When I am living in the Midlands
  That are sodden and unkind,
I light my lamp in the evening :
  My work is left behind ;
And the great hills of the South Country
  Come back into my mind.

The great hills of the South Country
  They stand along the sea ;
And it's there walking in the high woods
  That I could wish to be,
And the men that were boys when I was a boy
  Walking alone with me.

The men that live in North England
  I saw them for a day :
Their hearts are set upon the waste fells,
  Their skies are fast and grey ;
From their castle-walls a man may see
  The mountains far away.

The men that live in West England
  They see the Severn strong,
A-rolling on rough water brown
  Light aspen leaves along.
They have the secret of the Rocks,
  And the oldest kind of song.

But the men that live in the South Country
  Are the kindest and most wise,
They get their laughter from the loud surf,
  And the faith in their happy eyes
Comes surely from our Sister the Spring
  When over the sea she flies ;
The violets suddenly bloom at her feet,
  She blesses us with surprise.

I never get between the pines
  But I smell the Sussex air ;
Nor I never come on a belt of sand
  But my home is there.
And along the sky the line of the Downs
  So noble and so bare.

A lost thing could I never find,
  Nor a broken thing mend :
And I fear I shall be all alone
  When I get towards the end.
Who will there be to comfort me
  Or who will be my friend ?

I will gather and carefully make my friends
  Of the men of the Sussex Weald,
They watch the stars from silent folds,
  They stiffly plough the field,
By them and the God of the South Country
  My poor soul shall be healed.

If I ever become a rich man,
  Or if ever I grow to be old,
I will build a house with deep thatch
  To shelter me from the cold,
And there shall the Sussex songs be sung
  And the story of Sussex told.

I will hold my house in the high wood
  Within a walk of the sea,
And the men that were boys when I was a boy
  Shall sit and drink with me.

HILAIRE BELLOC

THE RECALL

I am the land of their fathers.
In me the virtue stays.
I will bring back my children,
After certain days.

Under their feet in the grasses
My clinging magic runs.
They shall return as strangers,
They shall remain as sons.

Over their heads in the branches
Of their new-bought ancient trees,
I weave an incantation
And draw them to my knees.

Scent of smoke in the evening,
Smell of rain in the night,
The hours, the days and the seasons,
Order their souls aright;

Till I make plain the meaning
Of all my thousand years—
Till I fill their hearts with knowledge,
While I fill their eyes with tears.

RUDYARD KIPLING

IN ROMNEY MARSH

As I went down to Dymchurch Wall
  I heard the South sing o'er the land;
I saw the yellow sunlight fall
  On knolls where Norman churches stand.

And ringing shrilly, taut and lithe,
  Within the wind a core of sound,
The wire from Romney town to Hythe
  Alone its airy journey wound.

A veil of purple vapour flowed
  And trailed its fringe along the Straits;
The upper air like sapphire glowed;
  And roses filled Heaven's central gates.

Masts in the offing wagged their tops;
  The swinging waves pealed on the shore;
The saffron beach, all diamond drops
  And beads of surge, prolonged the roar.

As I came up from Dymchurch Wall,
  I saw above the Downs' low crest
The crimson brands of sunset fall,
  Flicker and fade from out the west.

Night sank: like flakes of silver fire
  The stars in one great shower came down;
Shrill blew the wind; and shrill the wire
  Rang out from Hythe to Romney town.

The darkly shining salt sea drops
  Streamed as the waves clashed on the shore;
The beach, with all its organ stops
  Pealing again, prolonged the roar.

JOHN DAVIDSON

IT WAS THE LOVELY MOON

It was the lovely moon—she lifted
Slowly her white brow among
Bronze cloud-waves that ebbed and drifted
Faintly, faintlier afar.
Calm she looked, yet pale with wonder,
Sweet in unwonted thoughtfulness,
Watching the earth that dwindled under
Faintly, faintlier afar.
It was the lovely moon that lover-like
Hovered over the wandering, tired
Earth, her bosom grey and dove-like,
Hovering beautiful as a dove . . .
The lovely moon :—her soft light falling
Lightly on roof and poplar and pine—
Tree to tree whispering and calling,
Wonderful in the silvery shine
Of the round, lovely, thoughtful moon.

JOHN FREEMAN

THE EARLY MORNING

The moon on the one hand, the dawn on the other :
The moon is my sister, the dawn is my brother.
The moon on my left and the dawn on my right,
My brother, good morning : my sister, good night.

HILAIRE BELLOC

DAYS TOO SHORT

When primroses are out in Spring,
And small, blue violets come between ;
When merry birds sing on boughs green,
And rills, as soon as born, must sing ;

When butterflies will make side-leaps,
As though escaped from Nature's hand
Ere perfect quite ; and bees will stand
Upon their heads in fragrant deeps ;

When small clouds are so silvery white
Each seems a broken rimmèd moon—
When such things are, this world too soon,
or me, doth wear the veil of Night.

W. H. DAVIES

THE MAY-TREE

The May-tree on the hill
Stands in the night
So fragrant and so still
So dusky white,

That, stealing from the wood
In that sweet air,
You'd think Diana stood
Before you there.

If it be so, her bloom
Trembles with bliss,
She waits across the gloom
Her shepherd's kiss.

Touch her. A bird will start
From these pure snows,—
The dark and fluttering heart
Endymion knows.

ALFRED NOYES

THE CHESTNUT CASTS HIS FLAMBEAUX

The chestnut casts his flambeaux, and the flowers
  Stream from the hawthorn on the wind away,
The doors clap to, the pane is blind with showers.
  Pass me the can, lad ; there's an end of May.

There's one spoilt spring to scant our mortal lot,
  One season ruined of our little store.
May will be fine next year as like as not :
  Oh ay, but then we shall be twenty-four.

We for a certainty are not the first
  Have sat in taverns while the tempest hurled
Their hopeful plans to emptiness, and cursed
  Whatever brute and blackguard made the world.

It is in truth iniquity on high
  To cheat our sentenced souls of aught they crave,
And mar the merriment as you and I
  Fare on our long fool's-errand to the grave.

Iniquity it is ; but pass the can.
  My lad, no pair of kings our mothers bore ;
Our only portion is the estate of man :
  We want the moon, but we shall get no more.

If here to-day the cloud of thunder lours,
  To-morrow it will hie on far behests ;
The flesh will grieve on other bones than ours
  Soon, and the soul will mourn in other breasts.

The troubles of our proud and angry dust
  Are from eternity, and shall not fail.
Bear them we can, and if we can we must.
  Shoulder the sky, my lad, and drink your ale.

A. E. HOUSMAN

THE PLOUGHMAN

Under the long fell's stony eaves
The ploughman, going up and down,
Ridge after ridge man's tide-mark leaves,
And turns the hard grey soil to brown.

Striding, he measures out the earth
In lines of life, to rain and sun;
And every year that comes to birth
Sees him still striding on and on.

The seasons change, and then return;
Yet still, in blind unsparing ways,
However I may shrink or yearn,
The ploughman measures out my days.

His acre brought forth roots last year;
This year it bears the gleamy grain;
Next Spring shall seedling grass appear:
Then roots and corn and grass again.

Five times the young corn's pallid green
I have seen spread and change and thrill;
Five times the reapers I have seen
Go creeping up the far-off hill:

And, as the unknowing ploughman climbs
Slowly and inveterately,
I wonder long how many times
The corn will spring again for me.

GORDON BOTTOMLEY

THE PRAISE OF DUST

'What of vile dust?' the preacher said.
  Methought the whole world woke,
The dead stone lived beneath my foot,
  And my whole body spoke.

'You, that play tyrant to the dust,
  And stamp its wrinkled face,
This patient star that flings you not
  Far into homeless space,

'Come down out of your dusty shrine
  The living dust to see,
The flowers that at your sermon's end
  Stand blazing silently.

'Rich white and blood-red blossom; stones,
  Lichens like fire encrust;
A gleam of blue, a glare of gold,
  The vision of the dust.

'Pass them all by: till, as you come
  Where, at a city's edge,
Under a tree—I know it well—
  Under a lattice hedge,

'The sunshine falls on one brown head.
  You, too, O cold of clay,
Eater of stones, may haply hear
  The trumpets of that day

'When God to all His paladins
  By His own splendour swore
To make a fairer face than heaven,
  Of dust and nothing more.'

G. K. CHESTERTON

THE DONKEY

When fishes flew and forests walked
And figs grew upon thorn,
Some moment when the moon was blood
Then surely I was born;

With monstrous head and sickening cry
And ears like errant wings,
The devil's walking parody
On all four-footed things.

The tattered outlaw of the earth,
Of ancient, crooked will;
Starve, scourge, deride me: I am dumb,
I keep my secret still.

Fools! For I also had my hour;
One far fierce hour and sweet:
There was a shout about my ears,
And palms before my feet.

G. K. CHESTERTON

THE KINGDOM OF GOD

'In no strange land'

O world invisible, we view thee,
O world intangible, we touch thee,
O world unknowable, we know thee,
Inapprehensible, we clutch thee!

Does the fish soar to find the ocean,
The eagle plunge to find the air—
That we ask of the stars in motion
If they have rumour of thee there?

Not where the wheeling systems darken,
And our benumbed conceiving soars!—
The drift of pinions, would we hearken,
Beats at our own clay-shuttered doors.

The angels keep their ancient places;—
Turn but a stone, and start a wing!
'Tis ye, 'tis your estrangèd faces,
That miss the many-splendoured thing.

But (when so sad thou canst not sadder)
Cry;—and upon thy so sore loss
Shall shine the traffic of Jacob's ladder
Pitched betwixt Heaven and Charing Cross.

FRANCIS THOMPSON

THE WATERSHED

Lines written between Munich and Verona

Black mountains pricked with pointed pine
  A melancholy sky.
Out-distanced was the German vine,
  The sterile fields lay high.
From swarthy Alps I travelled forth
Aloft; it was the north, the north;
  Bound for the Noon was I.

I seemed to breast the streams that day;
  I met, opposed, withstood
The northward rivers on their way,
  My heart against the flood—
My heart that pressed to rise and reach,
And felt the love of altering speech,
  Of frontiers, in its blood.

But O the unfolding South! the burst
  Of summer! O to see
Of all the southward brooks the first!
  The travelling heart went free
With endless streams; that strife was stopped;
And down a thousand vales I dropped,
  I flowed to Italy.

ALICE MEYNELL

PORT OF HOLY PETER

The blue laguna rocks and quivers,
  Dull gurgling eddies twist and spin,
The climate does for people's livers,
  It's a nasty place to anchor in
    Is Spanish port,
    Fever port,
    Port of Holy Peter.

The town begins on the sea-beaches,
  And the town's mad with the stinging flies,
The drinking water's mostly leeches,
  It's a far remove from Paradise
    Is Spanish port,
    Fever port,
    Port of Holy Peter.

There's sand-bagging and throat-slitting,
  And quiet graves in the sea slime,
Stabbing, or course, and rum-hitting,
  Dirt, and drink, and stink, and crime,
    In Spanish port,
    Fever port,
    Port of Holy Peter.

All the day the wind's blowing
  From the thick swamp below the hills,
All the night the plague's growing,
  And the dawn brings the fever chills,
    In Spanish port,
    Fever port,
    Port of Holy Peter.

You get a thirst there's no slaking,
  You get the chills and fever-shakes,
Tongue yellow and head aching,
  And then the sleep that never wakes.
And all the year the heat's baking,
  The sea rots and the earth quakes,
    In Spanish port,
    Fever port,
    Port of Holy Peter.

JOHN MASEFIELD

SWEET STAY-AT-HOME

Sweet Stay-at-home, sweet Well-content,
Thou knowest of no strange continent:
Thou hast not felt thy bosom keep
A gentle motion with the deep;
Thou hast not sailed in Indian seas,
Where scent comes forth in every breeze.
Thou hast not seen the rich grape grow
For miles, as far as eyes can go;
Thou hast not seen a summer's night
When maids could sew by a worm's light;
Nor the North Sea in spring send out
Bright hues that like birds flit about
In solid cages of white ice—
Sweet Stay-at-home, sweet Love-one-place.
Thou hast not seen black fingers pick
White cotton when the bloom is thick,
Nor heard black throats in harmony;
Nor hast thou sat on stones that lie
Flat on the earth, that once did rise
To hide proud kings from common eyes;
Thou hast not seen plains full of bloom
Where green things had such little room
They pleased the eye like fairer flowers—
Sweet Stay-at-home, all these long hours.
Sweet Well-content, sweet Love-one-place,
Sweet, simple maid, bless thy dear face;
For thou hast made more homely stuff
Nurture thy gentle self enough;
I love thee for a heart that's kind—
Not for the knowledge in thy mind.

W. H. DAVIES

LEPANTO

White founts falling in the courts of the sun,
And the Soldan of Byzantium is smiling as they run ;
There is laughter like the fountains in that face of all men feared,
It stirs the forest darkness, the darkness of his beard,
It curls the blood-red crescent, the crescent of his lips,
For the inmost sea of all the earth is shaken with his ships.
They have dared the white republics up the capes of Italy,
They have dashed the Adriatic round the Lion of the Sea,
And the Pope has cast his arms abroad for agony and loss,
And called the kings of Christendom for swords about the Cross,
The cold queen of England is looking in the glass ;
The shadow of the Valois is yawning at the Mass ;
From evening isles fantastical rings faint the Spanish gun,
And the Lord upon the Golden Horn is laughing in the sun.

Dim drums throbbing, in the hills half heard,
Where only on a nameless throne a crownless prince has stirred,
Where, risen from a doubtful seat and half-attainted stall,
The last knight of Europe takes weapons from the wall,
The last and lingering troubadour to whom the bird has sung,
That once went singing southward when all the world was young,
In that enormous silence, tiny and unafraid,
Comes up along a winding road the noise of the Crusade.
Strong gongs groaning as the guns boom far,
Don John of Austria is going to the war,
Stiff flags straining in the night-blasts cold
In the gloom black-purple, in the glint old-gold,
Torchlight crimson on the copper kettle-drums,
Then the tuckets, then the trumpets, the cannon, and he comes.
Don John laughing in the brave beard curled,
Spurning of his stirrups like the thrones of all the world,

Holding his head up for a flag of all the free.
Love-light of Spain—hurrah!
Death-light of Africa!
Don John of Austria
Is riding to the sea.

Mahound is in his paradise above the evening star,
(*Don John of Austria is going to the war.*)
He moves a mighty turban on the timeless houri's knees,
His turban that is woven of the sunset and the seas.
He shakes the peacock gardens as he rises from his ease,
And he strides among the tree-tops and is taller than the
trees,
And his voice through all the garden is a thunder sent to
bring
Black Azrael and Ariel and Ammon on the wing.
Giants and the Genii,
Multiplex of wing and eye,
Whose strong obedience broke the sky
When Solomon was king.

They rush in red and purple from the red clouds of the
morn,
From temples where the yellow gods shut up their eyes in
scorn;
They rise in green robes roaring from the green hells of
the sea
Where fallen skies and evil hues and eyeless creatures be;
On them the sea-valves cluster and the grey sea-forests curl,
Splashed with a splendid sickness, the sickness of the pearl;
They swell in sapphire smoke out of the blue cracks of the
ground,—
They gather and they wonder and give worship to Mahound.
And he saith, 'Break up the mountains where the hermit-
folk can hide,
And sift the red and silver sands lest bone of saint abide,
And chase the Giaours flying night and day, not giving rest,
For that which was our trouble comes again out of the west.
We have set the seal of Solomon on all things under sun,
Of knowledge and of sorrow and endurance of things done,

But a noise is in the mountains, in the mountains, and I know
The voice that shook our palaces—four hundred years ago:
It is he that saith not "Kismet"; it is he that knows not Fate;
It is Richard, it is Raymond, it is Godfrey in the gate!
It is he whose loss is laughter when he counts the wager worth,
Put down your feet upon him, that our peace be on the earth.'
For he heard drums groaning and he heard guns jar,
(*Don John of Austria is going to the war.*)
Sudden and still—hurrah!
Bolt from Iberia!
Don John of Austria
Is gone by Alcalar.

St. Michael's on his Mountain in the sea-roads of the north,
(*Don John of Austria is girt and going forth.*)
Where the grey seas glitter and the sharp tides shift
And the sea folk labour and the red sails lift.
He shakes his lance of iron and he claps his wings of stone;
The noise is gone through Normandy; the noise is gone alone;
The North is full of tangled things and texts and aching eyes,
And dead is all the innocence of anger and surprise,
And Christian killeth Christian in a narrow dusty room,
And Christian dreadeth Christ that hath a newer face of doom,
And Christian hateth Mary that God kissed in Galilee,
But Don John of Austria is riding to the sea.
Don John calling through the blast and the eclipse,
Crying with the trumpet, with the trumpet of his lips,
Trumpet that sayeth ha!
Domino gloria!
Don John of Austria
Is shouting to the ships.
King Philip's in his closet with the Fleece about his neck,
(*Don John of Austria is armed upon the deck.*)
The walls are hung with velvet that is black and soft as sin,
And little dwarfs creep out of it and little dwarfs creep in.
He holds a crystal phial that has colours like the moon,

He touches, and it tingles, and he trembles very soon,
And his face is as a fungus of a leprous white and grey
Like plants in the high houses that are shuttered from the day,
And death is in the phial, and the end of noble work,
But Don John of Austria has fired upon the Turk.
Don John's hunting, and his hounds have bayed—
Booms away past Italy the rumour of his raid.
Gun upon gun, ha ! ha !
Gun upon gun, hurrah !
Don John of Austria
Has loosed the cannonade.

The Pope was in his chapel before day or battle broke,
(*Don John of Austria is hidden in the smoke.*)
The hidden room in man's house where God sits all the year,
The secret window whence the world looks small and very
dear.
He sees as in a mirror on the monstrous twilight sea
The crescent of his cruel ships whose name is mystery ;
They fling great shadows foe-wards, making Cross and
Castle dark,
They veil the plumèd lions on the galleys of St. Mark ;
And above the ships are palaces of brown, black-bearded
chiefs,
And below the ships are prisons, where with multitudinous
griefs,
Christian captives sick and sunless, all a labouring race repines
Like a race in sunken cities, like a nation in the mines.
They are lost like slaves that sweat, and in the skies of
morning hung
The stairways of the tallest gods when tyranny was young.
They are countless, voiceless, hopeless as those fallen or
fleeing on
Before the high King's horses in the granite of Babylon.
And many a one grows witless in his quiet room in hell
Where a yellow face looks inward through the lattice of his
cell,
And he finds his God forgotten, and he seeks no more a
sign—
(*But Don John of Austria has burst the battle-line !*)

Don John pounding from the slaughter-painted poop,
Purpling all the ocean like a bloody pirate's sloop,
Scarlet running over on the silvers and the golds,
Breaking of the hatches up and bursting of the holds,
Thronging of the thousands up that labour under sea
White for bliss and blind for sun and stunned for liberty.
Vivat Hispania!
Domino Gloria!
Don John of Austria
Has set his people free!

Cervantes on his galley sets the sword back in the sheath,
(*Don John of Austria rides homeward with a wreath.*)
And he sees across a weary land a straggling road in Spain,
Up which a lean and foolish knight forever rides in vain,
And he smiles, but not as Sultan's smile, and settles back the blade . . .
(*But Don John of Austria rides home from the Crusade.*)

G. K. CHESTERTON

TO-MORROW

Oh yesterday the cutting edge drank thirstily and deep,
The upland outlaws ringed us in and herded us as sheep,
They drove us from the stricken field and bayed us into keep;
But to-morrow,
By the living God, we'll try the game again!

Oh yesterday our little troup was ridden through and through,
Our swaying, tattered pennons fled, a broken, beaten few,
And all a summer afternoon they hunted us and slew;
But to-morrow,
By the living God, we'll try the game again!

And here upon the turret-top the bale-fire glowers red,
The wake-lights burn and drip about our hacked, disfigured dead,
And many a broken heart is here and many a broken head;
But to-morrow,
By the living God, we'll try the game again!

JOHN MASEFIELD

DINING-ROOM TEA

When you were there, and you, and you,
Happiness crowned the night ; I too,
Laughing and looking, one of all,
I watched the quivering lamplight fall
On plate and flowers and pouring tea
And cup and cloth ; and they and we
Flung all the dancing moments by
With jest and glitter. Lip and eye
Flashed on the glory, shone and cried,
Improvident, unmemoried ;
And fitfully and like a flame
The light of laughter went and came.
Proud in their careless transience moved
The changing faces that I loved.

Till suddenly, and otherwhence,
I looked upon your innocence.
For lifted clear and still and strange
From the dark woven flow of change
Under a vast and starless sky
I saw the immortal moment lie.
One instant I, an instant, knew
As God knows all. And it and you
I, above Time, oh, blind ! could see
In witless immortality.
I saw the marble cup ; the tea,
Hung on the air, an amber stream ;
I saw the fire's unglittering gleam,
The painted flame, the frozen smoke.
No more the flooding lamplight broke
On flying eyes and lips and hair ;
But lay, but slept unbroken there,
On stiller flesh, and body breathless,
And lips and laughter stayed and deathless,
And words on which no silence grew.
Light was more alive than you.

For suddenly, and otherwhence,
I looked on your magnificence.

I saw the stillness and the light,
And you, august, immortal, white,
Holy and strange; and every glint,
Posture and jest and thought and tint
Freed from the mask of transiency,
Triumphant in eternity,
Immote, immortal.

Dazed at length
Human eyes grew, mortal strength
Wearied; and Time began to creep.
Change closed about me like a sleep.
Light glinted on the eyes I loved.
The cup was filled. The bodies moved.
The drifting petal came to ground,
The laughter chimed its perfect round.
The broken syllable was ended.
And I, so certain and so friended,
How could I cloud, or how distress,
The heaven of your unconsciousness?
Or shake at Time's sufficient spell,
Stammering of lights unutterable?
The eternal holiness of you,
The timeless end, you never knew,
The peace that lay, the light that shone.
You never knew that I had gone
A million years away, and stayed
A million years. The laughter played
Unbroken round me; and the jest
Flashed on. And we that knew the best
Down wonderful hours grew happier yet.
I sang at heart, and talked, and eat,
And lived from laugh to laugh, I too,
When you were there, and you, and you.

RUPERT BROOKE

LIGHT HEART

Ears lack no food, for loaded Time
Spins taking tales from waifs of crime,
And hapless love wins luck for rhyme,—
Yet favour and bounty they blossom like flowers,
And begetting brings weeping on laughter like showers.
With both hands give then,
Let Light Heart live then,
For time-to-come's a sieve, when
Nothing shall through the web pass
Save freshness that groweth, is mown, and regroweth
like grass.

As bees with honey cram the hive
Sweet, loving lads do well to wive;
Where husband's kiss the toddlers thrive;
For favour and bounty they blossom like flowers,
And begetting brings weeping on laughter like showers.
With both hands give then,
Let Light Heart live then,
For time-to-come's a sieve, when
Nothing shall through the web pass
Save freshness that groweth, is mown, and regroweth
like grass.

No wall nor rafter cramps the sky;
Though airmen like the swallows fly,
The room for thought yet keeps man shy;
While favour and bounty they blossom like flowers,
And begetting brings weeping on laughter like showers.
With both hands give then,
Let Light Heart live then,
Since time-to-come's a sieve, when
Nothing shall through the web pass
Save freshness that groweth, is mown, and regroweth
like grass.

THOMAS STURGE MOORE

HEAVEN

Fish (fly-replete, in depth of June,
Dawdling away their wat'ry noon)
Ponder deep wisdom, dark or clear,
Each secret fishy hope or fear.
Fish say, they have their Stream and Pond;
But is there anything Beyond?
This life cannot be All, they swear,
For how unpleasant, if it were!
One may not doubt that, somehow, Good
Shall come of Water and of Mud;
And, sure, the reverent eye must see
A Purpose in Liquidity.
We darkly know, by Faith we cry,
The future is not Wholly Dry.
Mud unto mud!—Death eddies near—
Not here the appointed End, not here!
But somewhere, beyond Space and Time,
Is wetter water, slimier slime!
And there (they trust) there swimmeth One
Who swam ere rivers were begun,
Immense, of fishy form and mind,
Squamous, omnipotent, and kind;
And under that Almighty Fin
The littlest fish may enter in.
Oh! never fly conceals a hook,
Fish say, in the Eternal Brook,
But more than mundane weeds are there,
And mud, celestially fair;
Fat caterpillars drift around,
And Paradisal grubs are found;
Unfading moths, immortal flies,
And the worm that never dies.
And in that Heaven of all their wish,
There shall be no more land, say fish.

RUPERT BROOKE

FLYCATCHERS

Sweet pretty fledglings, perched on the rail arow,
Expectantly happy, where ye can watch below
Your parents a-hunting i' the meadow grasses
All the gay morning to feed you with flies;

Ye recall me a time sixty summers ago,
When, a young chubby chap, I sat just so
With others on a school-form rank'd in a row,
Not less eager and hungry than you, I trow,
With intelligences agape and eyes aglow,
While an authoritative old wise-acre
Stood over us and from a desk fed us with flies.

Dead flies—such as litter the library south-window,
That buzzed at the panes until they fell stiff-baked on the sill,
Or all roll'd up asleep i' the blinds at sunrise,
Or wafer'd flat in a shrunken folio.

A dry biped he was, nurtured likewise
On skins and skeletons, stale from top to toe
With all manner of rubbish and all manner of lies.

ROBERT BRIDGES

THE EXAMPLE

Here's an example from
  A Butterfly;
That on a rough, hard rock
  Happy can lie;
Friendless and all alone
On this unsweetened stone.

Now let my bed be hard,
  No care take I;
I'll make my joy like this
  Small Butterfly;
Whose happy heart has power
To make a stone a flower.

W. H. DAVIES

CHEDDAR PINKS

Mid the squander'd colour
  idling as I lay
Reading the Odyssey
  in my rock-garden
I espied the cluster'd
  tufts of Cheddar pinks
Burgeoning with promise
  of their scented bloom
All the modish motley
  of their bloom to-be
Thrust up in narrow buds
  on the slender stalks
Thronging springing urgent
  hasting (so I thought)
As if they feared to be
  too late for summer—
Like schoolgirls overslept
  waken'd by the bell
Leaping from bed to don
  their muslin dresses
    On a May morning.

Then felt I like to one
  indulging in sin
(Whereto Nature is oft
  a blind accomplice)
Because my aged bones
  so enjoyed the sun
There as I lay along
  idling with my thoughts
Reading an old poet
  while the busy world
Toil'd moil'd fuss'd and scurried
  worried bought and sold
Plotted stole and quarrel'd
  fought and God knows what.
I had forgotten Homer
  dallying with my thoughts

Till I fell to making
  these little verses
Communing with my flowers
  in my rock-garden
    On a May morning.

ROBERT BRIDGES

THE TREES

O dreamy, gloomy, friendly Trees,
I came along your narrow track
To bring my gifts into your knees
And gifts did you give back;
For when I brought this heart that burns—
These thoughts that bitterly repine—
And laid them here among the ferns
And the hum of boughs divine
Ye, vastest breathers of the air,
Shook down with show and mighty poise
Your coolness on the human care,
Your wonder on its toys,
Your greenness on the heart's despair,
Your darkness on its noise.

HERBERT TRENCH

THUNDERSTORMS

My mind has thunderstorms,
  That brood for heavy hours:
Until they rain me words,
  My thoughts are drooping flowers
And sulking, silent birds.

Yet come, dark thunderstorms,
  And brood your heavy hours;
For when you rain me words
  My thoughts are dancing flowers
And joyful singing birds.

W. H. DAVIES

THE RAIN

I hear leaves drinking rain ;
   I hear rich leaves on top
Giving the poor beneath
   Drop after drop ;
'Tis a sweet noise to hear
These green leaves drinking near.

And when the Sun comes out,
   After this rain shall stop,
A wondrous light will fill
   Each dark, round drop ;
I hope the Sun shines bright ;
'Twill be a lovely sight.

W. H. DAVIES

THE KINGFISHER

It was the rainbow gave thee birth,
   And left thee all her lovely hues ;
And, as her mother's name was Tears,
   So runs it in thy blood to choose
For haunts the lonely pools, and keep
In company with trees that weep.

Go you and, with such glorious hues,
   Live with proud Peacocks in green parks ;
On Lawns as smooth as shining glass,
   Let every feather show its marks ;
Get thee on boughs and clap thy wings
Before the windows of proud kings.

Nay, lovely Bird, thou art not vain ;
   Thou hast no proud, ambitious mind ;
I also love a quiet place
   That's green, away from all mankind ;
A lonely pool, and let a tree
Sigh with her bosom over me.

W. H. DAVIES

THE SHELL

I

And then I pressed the shell
Close to my ear,
And listened well.

And straightway, like a bell,
Came low and clear
The slow, sad murmur of far distant seas

Whipped by an icy breeze
Upon a shore
Wind-swept and desolate.

It was a sunless strand that never bore
The footprint of a man,
Nor felt the weight

Since time began
Of any human quality or stir,
Save what the dreary winds and wave incur.

II

And in the hush of waters was the sound
Of pebbles, rolling round;
For ever rolling, with a hollow sound:

And bubbling sea-weeds, as the waters go,
Swish to and fro
Their long cold tentacles of slimy grey:

There was no day;
Nor ever came a night
Setting the stars alight

To wonder at the moon:
Was twilight only, and the frightened croon,
Smitten to whimpers, of the dreary wind

And waves that journeyed blind . . .
And then I loosed my ear—Oh, it was sweet
To hear a cart go jolting down the street.

JAMES STEPHENS

SCHOOL'S OUT

Girls scream,
    Boys shout;
Dogs bark,
    School's out.

Cats run,
    Horses shy;
Into trees
    Birds fly.

Babes wake
    Open-eyed;
If they can,
    Tramps hide.

Old man,
    Hobble home;
Merry mites,
    Welcome.

W. H. DAVIES

A ST. HELENA LULLABY

'How far is St. Helena from a little child at play?'
What makes you want to wander there with all the world
        between?
Oh, Mother, call your son again or else he'll run away.
(*No one thinks of winter when the grass is green!*)

'How far is St. Helena from a fight in Paris Street?'
I haven't time to answer now—the men are falling fast.
The guns begin to thunder, and the drums begin to beat.
(*If you take the first step, you will take the last!*)

'How far is St. Helena from the field of Austerlitz?'
You couldn't hear me if I told—so loud the cannons roar.
But not so far for people who are living by their wits.
('*Gay go up*' *means* '*Gay go down*' *the wide world o'er!*)

'How far is St. Helena from an Emperor of France?'
I cannot see—I cannot tell—the crowns they dazzle so.
The Kings sit down to dinner, and the Queens stand up to dance.
(*After open weather you may look for snow!*)

'How far is St. Helena from the Capes of Trafalgar?'
A longish way—a longish way—with ten year more to run.
It's South across the water underneath a falling star.
(*What you cannot finish you must leave undone!*)

'How far is St. Helena from the Beresina Ice?'
An ill way—a chill way—the ice begins to crack.
But not so far for gentlemen who never took advice.
(*When you can't go forward you must e'en come back!*)

'How far is St. Helena from the field of Waterloo?'
A near way—a clear way—the ship will take you soon.
A pleasant place for gentlemen with little left to do.
(*Morning never tries you till the afternoon!*)

'How far from St. Helena to the Gate of Heaven's Grace?'
That no one knows—that no one knows—and no one ever will.
But fold your hands across your heart and cover up your face,
And after all your trapesings, child, lie still!

RUDYARD KIPLING

I LOOK INTO MY GLASS

I look into my glass
And view my wasting skin,
And say, ' Would God it came to pass
My heart had shrunk as thin ! '

For then, I, undistrest
By hearts grown cold to me,
Could lonely wait my endless rest
With equanimity.

But Time, to make me grieve,
Part steals, lets part abide ;
And shakes this fragile frame at eve
With throbbings of noontide.

THOMAS HARDY

EPITAPH

Sir, you should notice me : I am the Man :
I am Good Fortune : I am satisfied.
All I desired, more than I could desire,
I have : everything has gone right with me.
Life was a hiding-place that played me false ;
I croucht ashamed, and still was seen and scorned :
But now I am not seen. I was a fool,
And now I know what wisdom dare not know :
For I know Nothing. I was a slave, and now
I have ungoverned freedom, and the wealth
That cannot be conceived : for I have Nothing.
I lookt for beauty and I longed for rest,
And now I have perfection : nay, I am
Perfection : I am Nothing, I am dead.

LASCELLES ABERCROMBIE

AFTERWARDS

When the Present has latched its postern behind my
tremulous stay,
And the May month flaps its glad green leaves like wings,
Delicate-filmed as new-spun silk, will the neighbours say,
'He was a man who used to notice such things'?

If it be in the dusk when, like an eyelid's soundless blink
The dewfall-hawk comes crossing the shades to alight
Upon the wind-warped upland thorn, a gazer may think,
'To him this must have been a familiar sight.'

If I pass during some nocturnal blackness, mothy and warm,
When the hedgehog travels furtively over the lawn,
One may say, 'He strove that such innocent creatures should
come to no harm,
But he could do little for them; and now he is gone.'

If, when hearing that I have been stilled at last, they stand at
the door,
Watching the full-starred heavens that winter sees,
Will this thought rise on those who will meet my face no
more,
'He was one who had an eye for such mysteries'?

And will any say when my bell of quittance is heard in the
gloom,
And a crossing breeze cuts a pause in its outrollings,
Till they rise again, as they were a new bell's boom,
'He hears it not now, but used to notice such things'?

THOMAS HARDY

AUTOBIOGRAPHY

Wales England wed; so I was bred,
'twas merry London gave me breath.
I dreamt of love,—and fame: I strove:
but Ireland taught me love was best.
And Irish eyes, and London cries,
and streams of Wales, may tell the rest,
What more than these I asked of Life,
I am content to have from Death.

ERNEST RHYS

THE HAMMERS

Noise of hammers once I heard,
Many hammers, busy hammers,
Beating, shaping, night and day,
Shaping, beating dust and clay
To a palace ; saw it reared ;
Saw the hammers laid away.

And I listened, and I heard
Hammers beating, night and day,
In the palace newly reared,
Beating it to dust and clay :
Other hammers, muffled hammers,
Silent hammers of decay.

RALPH HODGSON

THE HILL

Breathless, we flung us on the windy hill,
  Laughed in the sun, and kissed the lovely grass.
  You said, ‘ Through glory and ecstasy we pass ;
Wind, sun, and earth remain, the birds sing still,
When we are old, are old . . . ’ ‘ And when we die
  All's over that is ours ; and life burns on
Through other lovers, other lips,’ said I,
  ‘ Heart of my heart, our heaven is now, is won ! ’

‘ We are Earth's best, that learnt her lesson here.
  Life is our cry. We kept the faith ! ’ we said ;
  ‘ We shall go down with unreluctant tread
Rose-crowned into the darkness ! ’ . . . Proud we were,
  And laughed, that had such brave true things to say.
  —And then you suddenly cried, and turned away.

RUPERT BROOKE

AUTUMN

There is a wind where the rose was ;
Cold rain where sweet grass was ;
　And clouds like sheep
　Stream o'er the steep
Grey skies where the lark was.

Nought gold where your hair was ;
Nought warm where your hand was ;
　But phantom, forlorn,
　Beneath the thorn,
Your ghost where your face was.

Sad winds where your voice was ;
Tears, tears where my heart was ;
　And ever with me,
　Child, ever with me,
Silence where hope was.

WALTER DE LA MARE

THE DANCER

The tall dancer dances
With slowly-taken breath :
In his feet music
And on his face death.

His face is a mask,
It is so still and white :
His withered eyes shut,
Unmindful of light.

The old fiddler fiddles
The merry *Silver Tip*
With softly-beating foot
And laughing eye and lip.

And round the dark walls
The people sit and stand,
Praising the art
Of the dancer of the land.

But he dances there
As if his kin were dead:
Clay in his thoughts,
And lightning in his tread!

JOSEPH CAMPBELL

I AM TIRED OF THE WIND

I am tired of the wind—
Oh, wind, wind, be quiet . . .
I am burdened by the days
Of wailing and long riot.
The heavy trees are thinned;
The clouds lose their ways . . .
There's no rest in my mind.

When the wind falls the rain falls;
The air has no more breath.
The ceaseless 'Hush' of rain
Is what eternity saith.
The hills grown near and tall
Let down a misty mane . . .
Endlessness weighs on all.

GORDON BOTTOMLEY

I HEAR AN ARMY CHARGING

I hear an army charging upon the land,
And the thunder of horses plunging, foam about their knees:
Arrogant, in black armour, behind them stand,
Disdaining the reins, with fluttering whips, the charioteers.

They cry unto the night their battle-name:
I moan in sleep when I hear afar their whirling laughter.
They cleave the gloom of dreams, a blinding flame,
Clanging, clanging upon the heart as upon an anvil.

They come shaking in triumph their long, green hair:
They come out of the sea and run shouting by the shore.
My heart, have you no wisdom thus to despair?
My love, my love, my love, why have you left me alone?

JAMES JOYCE

II

1914–1918

THE TRUMPET

Rise up, rise up,
And, as the trumpet blowing
Chases the dreams of men,
As the dawn glowing
The stars that left unlit
The land and water,
Rise up and scatter
The dew that covers
The print of last night's lovers—
Scatter it, scatter it !

While you are listening
To the clear horn,
Forget, men, everything
On this earth new-born,
Except that it is lovelier
Than any mysteries.
Open your eyes to the air
That has washed the eyes of the stars
Through all the dewy night :
Up with the light
To the old wars ;
Arise, arise !

EDWARD THOMAS

THE NEW HOUSE

Now first, as I shut the door,
    I was alone
In the new house; and the wind
    Began to moan.

Old at once was the house,
    And I was old;
My ears were teased with the dread
    Of what was foretold,

Nights of storm, days of mist, without end;
    Sad days when the sun
Shone in vain: old griefs and griefs
    Not yet begun.

All was foretold me; naught
    Could I foresee;
But I learnt how the wind would sound
    After these things should be.

EDWARD THOMAS

THE EXILE

I am that Adam who, with Snake for guest,
Hid anguished eyes upon Eve's piteous breast.
I am that Adam who, with broken wings,
Fled from the Seraph's brazen trumpetings.
Betrayed and fugitive, I still must roam
A world where sin, and beauty, whisper of Home.

Oh, from wide circuit, shall at length I see
Pure daybreak lighten again on Eden's tree?
Loosed from remorse and hope and love's distress,
Enrobe me again in my lost nakedness?
No more with wordless grief a loved one grieve,
But to Heaven's nothingness re-welcome Eve?

WALTER DE LA MARE

SONNET

O little self, within whose smallness lies
All that man was, and is, and will become,
Atom unseen that comprehends the skies
And tells the tracks by which the planets roam;
That, without moving, knows the joy of wings,
The tiger's strength, the eagle's secrecy,
And in the hovel can consort with kings,
Or clothe a God with his own mystery.
O with what darkness do we cloak thy light,
What dusty folly gather thee for food,
Thou who alone art knowledge and delight,
The heavenly bread, the beautiful, the good.
O living self, O God, O morning star,
Give us thy light, forgive us what we are.

JOHN MASEFIELD

THE GLORY

The glory of the beauty of the morning,—
The cuckoo crying over the untouched dew;
The blackbird that has found it, and the dove
That tempts me on to something sweeter than love;
White clouds ranged even and fair as new-mown hay;
The heat, the stir, the sublime vacancy
Of sky and meadow and forest and my own heart:—
The glory invites me, yet it leaves me scorning
All I can ever do, all I can be,
Beside the lovely of motion, shape, and hue,
The happiness I fancy fit to dwell
In beauty's presence. Shall I now this day
Begin to seek as far as heaven, as hell,
Wisdom or strength to match this beauty, start
And tread the pale dust pitted with small dark drops,

In hope to find whatever it is I seek,
Hearkening to short-lived happy-seeming things
That we know naught of, in the hazel copse?
Or must I be content with discontent
As larks and swallows are perhaps with wings?
And shall I ask at the day's end once more
What beauty is, and what I can have meant
By happiness? And shall I let all go,
Glad, weary, or both? Or shall I perhaps know
That I was happy oft, and oft before,
Awhile forgetting how I am fast pent,
How dreary-swift, with naught to travel to,
Is Time? I cannot bite the day to the core.

EDWARD THOMAS

IN THE SNOW

Hear how my friend the robin sings!
  That little hunchback in the snow,
As it comes down as fast as rain.
  The air is cold, the wind doth blow,
And still his heart can feel no pain.

And I, with heart as light as his,
  And to my ankles deep in snow,
Hold up a fist as cold as Death's,
  And into it I laugh and blow—
I laugh and blow my life's warm breath.

W. H. DAVIES

ROMANCE

When I was but thirteen or so
  I went into a golden land,
Chimborazo, Cotopaxi
  Took me by the hand.

My father died, my brother too,
  They passed like fleeting dreams.
I stood where Popocatapetl
  In the sunlight gleams.

I dimly heard the Master's voice
  And the boys' far-off play,
Chimborazo, Cotopaxi
  Had stolen me away.

I walked in a great golden dream
  To and fro from school—
Shining Popocatapetl
  The dusty streets did rule.

I walked home with a gold dark boy
  And never a word I'd say,
Chimborazo, Cotopaxi
  Had taken my speech away:

I gazed entranced upon his face
  Fairer than any flower—
O shining Popocatapetl,
  It was thy magic hour:

The houses, people, traffic, seemed
  Thin fading dreams by day,
Chimborazo, Cotopaxi
  They had stolen my soul away!

W. J. TURNER

ECSTASY

I saw a frieze on whitest marble drawn
Of boys who sought for shells along the shore,
Their white feet shedding pallor in the sea,
The shallow sea, the spring-time sea of green
That faintly creamed against the cold, smooth pebbles.

The air was thin, their limbs were delicate,
The wind had graven their small eager hands
To feel the forests and the dark nights of Asia
Behind the purple bloom of the horizon,
Where sails would float and slowly melt away.

Their naked, pure, and grave, unbroken silence
Filled the soft air as gleaming, limpid water
Fills a spring sky those days when rain is lying
In shattered bright pools on the wind-dried roads,
And their sweet bodies were wind-purified.

One held a shell unto his shell-like ear
And there was music carven in his face,
His eyes half-closed, his lips just breaking open
To catch the lulling, mazy, coralline roar
Of numberless caverns filled with singing seas.

And all of them were hearkening as to singing
Of far-off voices thin and delicate,
Voices too fine for any mortal mind
To blow into the whorls of mortal ears—
And yet those sounds flowed from their grave, sweet faces.

And as I looked I heard that delicate music,
And I became as grave, as calm, as still
As those carved boys. I stood upon that shore,
I felt the cool sea dream around my feet,
My eyes were staring at the far horizon:

And the wind came and purified my limbs,
And the stars came and set within my eyes,
And snowy clouds rested upon my shoulders,
And the blue sky shimmered deep within me,
And I sang like a carven pipe of music.

W. J. TURNER

LA FIGLIA CHE PIANGE

O quam te memorem virgo . . .

Stand on the highest pavement of the stair—
Lean on a garden urn—
Weave, weave the sunlight in your hair—
Clasp your flowers to you with a pained surprise—
Fling them to the ground and turn
With a fugitive resentment in your eyes :
But weave, weave the sunlight in your hair.

So I would have had him leave,
So I would have had her stand and grieve,
So he would have left
As the soul leaves the body torn and bruised,
As the mind deserts the body it has used.
I should find
Some way incomparably light and deft,
Some way we both should understand,
Simple and faithless as a smile and shake of the hand.

She turned away, but with the autumn weather
Compelled my imagination many days,
Many days and many hours :
Her hair over her arms and her arms full of flowers.
And I wonder how they should have been together !
I should have lost a gesture and a pose.
Sometimes these cogitations still amaze
The troubled midnight and the noon's repose.

T. S. ELIOT

SOWING

It was a perfect day
For sowing ; just
As sweet and dry was the ground
As tobacco-dust.

I tasted deep the hour
Between the far
Owl's chuckling first soft cry
And the first star.

A long stretched hour it was ;
Nothing undone
Remained ; the early seeds
All safely sown.

And now, hark at the rain,
Windless and light,
Half a kiss, half a tear,
Saying good-night.

EDWARD THOMAS

THE GREEN ROADS

The green roads that end in the forest
Are strewn with white goose feathers this June,

Like marks left behind by someone gone to the forest
To show his track. But he has never come back.

Down each green road a cottage looks at the forest.
Round one the nettle towers ; two are bathed in flowers.

An old man along the green road to the forest
Strays from one, from another a child alone.

In the thicket bordering the forest,
All day long a thrush twiddles his song.

It is old, but the trees are young in the forest:
All but one like a castle keep, in the middle deep.

That oak saw the ages pass in the forest:
They were a host, but their memories are lost,

For the tree is dead: all things forget the forest
Excepting perhaps me, when now I see

The old man, the child, the goose feathers at the edge of
    the forest,
And hear all day long the thrush repeat his song.

EDWARD THOMAS

OCTOBER

The green elm with the one great bough of gold
Lets leaves into the grass slip, one by one,—
The short hill grass, the mushrooms small, milk-white,
Harebell and scabious and tormentil,
That blackberry and gorse, in dew and sun,
Bow down to; and the wind travels too light
To shake the fallen birch leaves from the fern;
The gossamers wander at their own will.
At heavier steps than birds' the squirrels scold.
The rich scene has grown fresh again and new
As Spring and to the touch is not more cool
Than it is warm to the gaze; and now I might
As happy be as earth is beautiful,
Were I some other or with earth could turn
In alternation of violet and rose,
Harebell and snowdrop, at their season due,
And gorse that has not time not to be gay.
But if this be not happiness,—who knows?
Some day I shall think this a happy day,
And this mood by the name of melancholy
Shall not more blackened and obscuréd be.

EDWARD THOMAS

THE MILL-POND

The sun blazed while the thunder yet
Added a boom :
A wagtail flickered bright over
The mill-pond's gloom :

Less than the cooing in the alder
Isles of the pool
Sounded the thunder through that plunge
Of waters cool.

Scared starlings on the aspen tip
Past the black mill
Outchattered the stream and the next roar
Far on the hill.

As my feet dangling teased the foam
That slid below,
A girl came out. 'Take care ! ' she said—
Ages ago.

She startled me, standing quite close
Dressed all in white ;
Ages ago I was angry till
She passed from sight.

Then the storm burst, and as I crouched
To shelter, how
Beautiful and kind, too, she seemed,
As she does now !

EDWARD THOMAS

THE MOON

Thy beauty haunts me heart and soul,
   Oh thou fair Moon, so close and bright;
Thy beauty makes me like the child
   That cries aloud to own thy light:
The little child that lifts each arm
To press thee to her bosom warm.

Though there are birds that sing this night
   With thy white beams across their throats,
Let my deep silence speak for me
   More than for them their sweetest notes:
Who worships thee till music fails
Is greater than thy nightingales.

W. H. DAVIES

A GREAT TIME

Sweet Chancc, that led my steps abroad,
   Beyond the town, where wild flowers grow—
A rainbow and a cuckoo, Lord,
   How rich and great the times are now!
         Know, all ye sheep
         And cows, that keep
On staring that I stand so long
   In grass that's wet from heavy rain—
A rainbow and a cuckoo's song
   May never come together again;
         May never come
         This side the tomb.

W. H. DAVIES

BRIGHT CLOUDS

Bright clouds of may
Shade half the pond.
Beyond,
All but one bay
Of emerald
Tall reeds
Like criss-cross bayonets
Where a bird once called,
Lies bright as the sun.
No one heeds.
The light wind frets
And drifts the scum
Of may-blossom.
Till the moorhen calls
Again
Naught's to be done
By birds or men.
Still the may falls.

EDWARD THOMAS

TALL NETTLES

Tall nettles cover up, as they have done
These many springs, the rusty harrow, the plough
Long worn out, and the roller made of stone :
Only the elm butt tops the nettles now.

This corner of the farmyard I like most :
As well as any bloom upon a flower
I like the dust on nettles, never lost
Except to prove the sweetness of a shower.

EDWARD THOMAS

IN THE CAVES OF AUVERGNE

He carved the red deer and the bull
  Upon the smooth cave rock,
Returned from war with belly full,
  And scarred with many a knock,
He carved the red deer and the bull
  Upon the smooth cave rock.

The stars flew by the cave's wide door,
  The clouds wild trumpets blew,
Trees rose in wild dreams from the floor,
  Flowers with dream faces grew
Up to the sky, and softly hung
  Golden and white and blue.

The woman ground her heap of corn,
  Her heart a guarded fire;
The wind played in his trembling soul
  Like a hand upon a lyre,
The wind drew faintly on the stone
  Symbols of his desire:

The red deer of the forests dark,
  Whose antlers cut the sky,
That vanishes into the mirk
  And like a dream flits by,
And by an arrow slain at last
  Is but the wind's dark body.

The bull that stands in marshy lakes
  As motionless and still
As a dark rock jutting from a plain
  Without a tree or hill;
The bull that is the sign of life,
  Its sombre, phallic will.

And from the dead white eyes of them
  The wind springs up anew,
It blows upon the trembling heart,
  And bull and deer renew
Their flitting life in the dim past
  When that dead Hunter drew.

I sit beside him in the night,
  And, fingering his red stone,
I chase through endless forests dark,
  Seeking that thing unknown,
That which is not red deer or bull,
  But which by them was shown:

By those stiff shapes in which he drew
  His soul's exalted cry,
When flying down the forest dark
  He slew and knew not why,
When he was filled with song, and strength
  Flowed to him from the sky.

The wind blows from red deer and bull,
  The clouds wild trumpets blare,
Trees rise in wild dreams from the earth,
  Flowers with dream faces stare;
O, *Hunter, your own shadow stands*
  Within your forest lair!

W. J. TURNER

THE STINGING NETTLE

With seed the sowers scatter
The furrows as they go;
Poor lads, 'tis little matter
How many sorts they sow,
For only one will grow.

The charlock on the fallow
Will take the traveller's eyes,
And gild the ploughland sallow
With flowers before it dies,
But twice 'twill not arise.

The stinging nettle only
Will still be found to stand:
The numberless, the lonely,
The thronger of the land,
The leaf that hurts the hand.

It thrives, come sun, come showers,
Blow east, blow west, it springs;
It peoples towns, and towers
Above the courts of Kings,
And touch it and it stings.

A. E. HOUSMAN

IN SEPTEMBER

Still are the meadowlands, and still
Ripens the upland corn,
And over the brown gradual hill
The moon has dipped a horn.

The voices of the dear unknown
With silent hearts now call,
My rose of youth is overblown
And trembles to the fall.

My song forsakes me like the birds
That leave the rain and grey,
I hear the music of the words
My lute can never say.

FRANCIS LEDWIDGE

PEACE

Now, God be thanked Who has matched us with His hour,
And caught our youth, and wakened us from sleeping,
With hand made sure, clear eye, and sharpened power,
To turn, as swimmers into cleanness leaping,
Glad from a world grown old and cold and weary,
Leave the sick hearts that honour could not move,
And half-men, and their dirty songs and dreary,
And all the little emptiness of love!

Oh, we, who have known shame, we have found release there,
Where there's no ill, no grief, but sleep has mending,
Naught broken save this body, lost but breath;
Nothing to shake the laughing heart's long peace there
But only agony, and that has ending;
And the worst friend and enemy is but Death.

RUPERT BROOKE

EPITAPH ON AN ARMY OF MERCENARIES

These, in the day when heaven was falling,
The hour when earth's foundations fled,
Followed their mercenary calling
And took their wages and are dead.

Their shoulders held the sky suspended;
They stood, and earth's foundations stay;
What God abandoned, these defended,
And saved the sum of things for pay.

A. E. HOUSMAN

IN TIME OF 'THE BREAKING OF NATIONS' (1915)

Only a man harrowing clods
 In a slow silent walk
With an old horse that stumbles and nods
 Half asleep as they stalk.

Only thin smoke without flame
 From the heaps of couch-grass ;
Yet this will go onward the same
 Though Dynasties pass.

Yonder a maid and her wight
 Come whispering by :
War's annals will cloud into night
 Ere their story die.

THOMAS HARDY

FROM 'THE SONG OF THE PLOW'

THE MAN ON THE HILL

Under the sun on the gray hill,
 At breakfast campt behind the hedge,
 There ate he, there eats he still
Bread and bacon on the knife's edge.
 Blow the wind chill, be sky of lead,
 Or let the sun burn e'er the ridge,
Or be the cloudy fleeces spread,
 Or let rain drive, or snow come dry
 What time the blackthorn flower is shed
Like puffs of smoke on the blue sky—
 There sits he now as he sat then
 And watches how the year goes by,
And sees the world God made for men
 As little for them as it was
 In those old days of Cæsar's when

Lord Christ came riding on an ass,
  Borrowed from out some friendly stall,
  Or lifted from the common grass
And set to this new festival.
  So then to work, with heavy foot,
  To rouse his horses with a call;
And slow as they he puts them to't,
  To hale the plow on the stony down
  Thro' marl and flint, thro' stock and root,
Where the rooks cloud the strip of brown
  And querulous peewits wheel and flock:
  Behold them on the sky-line thrown
Like giant shapes of riven rock,
  He and his team on the world's rim
  Creeping like the hands of a clock.
Or in wet meadows plashy and dim
  When winter winds blow shrill and keen,
  See him bank up the warp and swim
The eddying water over the green;
  Or follow up the hill the sheep
  To where the kestrels soar and lean,
And from her form the hare doth leap
  Quick and short, and lightly flies
  Before him up the grassy steep
Where cloakt and crookt he climbs. His eyes,
  Seeing all things, and seeking none,
  Are very patient and weather-wise.
The clearest eyesight under the sun
  He has, and holds the ancient way,
  The way his forefathers have gone,
And deems himself as wise as they.

MAURICE HEWLETT

INTO BATTLE

1915

The naked earth is warm with Spring,
  And with green grass and bursting trees
Leans to the sun's gaze glorying,
  And quivers in the sunny breeze :

And Life is Colour and Warmth and Light,
  And a striving evermore for these ;
And he is dead who will not fight ;
  And who dies fighting has increase.

The fighting man shall from the sun
  Take warmth, and life from the glowing earth ;
Speed with the light-foot winds to run,
  And with the trees to newer birth ;
And find, when fighting shall be done,
  Great rest, and fullness after dearth.

All the bright company of Heaven
  Hold him in their high comradeship,
The Dog-star, and the Sisters Seven,
  Orion's Belt and sworded hip.

The woodland trees that stand together,
  They stand to him each one a friend ;
They gently speak in the windy weather ;
  They guide to valley and ridges' end.

The kestrel hovering by day,
  And the little owls that call by night,
Bid him be swift and keen as they,
  As keen of ear, as swift of sight.

The blackbird sings to him, 'Brother, brother,
  If this be the last song you shall sing,
Sing well, for you may not sing another ;
  Brother, sing.'

In dreary, doubtful waiting hours,
  Before the brazen frenzy starts,
The horses show him nobler powers ;—
  O patient eyes, courageous hearts !

And when the burning moment breaks,
  And all things else are out of mind,
And only Joy of Battle takes
  Him by the throat, and makes him blind,

Through joy and blindness he shall know,
  Not caring much to know, that still
Nor lead nor steel shall reach him, so
  That it be not the Destined Will.

The thundering line of battle stands,
  And in the air Death moans and sings ;
But Day shall clasp him with strong hands,
  And Night shall fold him in soft wings.

JULIAN GRENFELL

LOST IN FRANCE

JO'S REQUIEM

He had the plowman's strength
in the grasp of his hand :
He could see a crow
three miles away,
and the trout beneath the stone.
He could hear the green oats growing,
and the south-west wind making rain.
He could hear the wheel upon the hill
when it left the level road.
He could make a gate, and dig a pit,
And plow as straight as stone can fall.
And he is dead.

ERNEST RHYS

JULIAN GRENFELL

Because of you we will be glad and gay;
Remembering you, we will be brave and strong;
And hail the advent of each dangerous day,
And meet the last adventure with a song.
And, as you proudly gave your jewelled gift,
We'll give our lesser offering with a smile,
Nor falter on that path where, all too swift,
You led the way and leapt the golden stile.
Whether new paths, new heights to climb you find,
Or gallop through the unfooted asphodel,
We know you know we shall not lag behind,
Nor halt to waste a moment on a fear;
And you will speed us onward with a cheer
And wave beyond the stars that all is well.

MAURICE BARING

THE SOLDIER

If I should die, think only this of me:
 That there's some corner of a foreign field
That is for ever England. There shall be
 In that rich earth a richer dust concealed;
A dust whom England bore, shaped, made aware,
 Gave, once, her flowers to love, her ways to roam,
A body of England's, breathing English air,
 Washed by the rivers, blest by suns of home.

And think, this heart, all evil shed away,
 A pulse in the eternal mind, no less
 Gives somewhere back the thoughts by England given;
Her sights and sounds; dreams happy as her day;
 And laughter, learnt of friends; and gentleness,
 In hearts at peace, under an English heaven.

RUPERT BROOKE

ROUTE MARCH

All the hills and vales along
Earth is bursting into song,
And the singers are the chaps
Who are going to die perhaps.
    O sing, marching men,
    Till the valleys ring again.
    Give your gladness to earth's keeping,
    So be glad, when you are sleeping.

Cast away regret and rue,
Think what you are marching to.
Little live, great pass.
Jesus Christ and Barabbas
Were found the same day.
This died, that went his way.
    So sing with joyful breath.
    For why, you are going to death.
    Teeming earth will surely store
    All the gladness that you pour.

Earth that never doubts nor fears
Earth that knows of death, not tears,
Earth that bore with joyful ease
Hemlock for Socrates,
Earth that blossomed and was glad
'Neath the cross that Christ had
Shall rejoice and blossom too
When the bullet reaches you.
    Wherefore men, marching
    On the road to death, sing!
    Pour gladness on earth's head,
    So be merry, so be dead.

From the hills and valleys earth
Shouts back the sound of mirth,
Tramp of feet and lilt of song
Ringing all the road along.

All the music of their going,
Ringing, swinging, glad song-throwing,
Earth will echo still, when foot
Lies numb and voice mute.
On marching men, on
To the gates of death with song.
Sow your gladness for earth's reaping,
So you may be glad, though sleeping.
Strew your gladness on earth's bed,
So be merry, so be dead.

CHARLES SORLEY

A MOMENT'S INTERLUDE

One night I wandered alone from my comrades' huts ;
The grasshoppers chirped softly
In the warm misty evening ;
Bracken fronds beckoned from the darkness
With exquisite frail green fingers ;
The tree-gods muttered affectionately about me
And from the distance came the grumble of a kindly train.

I was so happy to be alone,
So full of love for the great speechless earth,
That I could have laid my cheek in the grasses
And caressed with my lips the hard sinewy body
Of Earth, the cherishing mistress of bitter lovers.

RICHARD ALDINGTON

DAWN ON THE SOMME

Last night rain fell over the scarred plateau,
And now from the dark horizon, dazzling, flies
Arrow on fire-plumed arrow to the skies,
Shot from the bright arc of Apollo's bow;
And from the wild and writhen waste below,
From flashing pools and mounds lit one by one,
Oh, is it mist, or are these companies
Of morning heroes who arise, arise
With thrusting arms, with limbs and hair aglow,
Toward the risen god, upon whose brow
Burns the gold laurel of all victories,
Hero and heroes' god, the invincible Sun?

ROBERT NICHOLS

THE TROOPS

Dim gradual thinning of the shapeless gloom
Shudders to drizzling daybreak that reveals
Disconsolate men who stamp their sodden boots
And turn dulled, sunken faces to the sky
Haggard and hopeless. They, who have beaten down
The stale despair of night, must now renew
Their desolation in the truce of dawn,
Murdering the livid hours that grope for peace.

Yet these, who cling to life with stubborn hands,
Can grin through storms of death and find a gap
In the clawed, cruel tangles of his defence.
They march from safety, and the bird-sung joy
Of grass-green thickets, to the land where all
Is ruin, and nothing blossoms but the sky
That hastens over them where they endure
Sad smoking, flat horizons, reeking woods,
And foundered trench-lines volleying doom for doom.

O my brave brown companions, when your souls
Flock silently away, and the eyeless dead
Shame the wild beast of battle on the ridge,
Death will stand grieving in that field of war
Since your unvanquished hardihood is spent.
And through some mooned Valhalla there will pass
Battalions and battalions, scarred from hell;
The unreturning army that was youth;
The legions who have suffered and are dust.

SIEGFRIED SASSOON

ASLEEP

Under his helmet, up against his pack,
After the many days of work and waking,
Sleep took him by the brow and laid him back.
And in the happy no-time of his sleeping,
Death took him by the heart. There was a quaking
Of the aborted life within him leaping . . .
Then chest and sleepy arms once more fell slack.
And soon the slow, stray blood came creeping
From the intrusive lead, like ants on track.

Whether his deeper sleep lie shaded by the shaking
Of great wings, and the thoughts that hung the stars,
High-pillowed on calm pillows of God's making
Above these clouds, these rains, these sleets of lead,
And these winds' scimitars;
—Or whether yet his thin and sodden head
Confuses more and more with the low mould,
His hair being one with the grey grass
And finished fields of autumns that are old . . .
Who knows? Who hopes? Who troubles? Let it pass!
He sleeps. He sleeps less tremulous, less cold,
Than we who must awake, and waking, say Alas!

WILFRED OWEN

THE DUG-OUT

Why do you lie with your legs ungainly huddled,
And one arm bent across your sullen cold
Exhausted face? It hurts my heart to watch you,
Deep-shadow'd from the candle's guttering gold;
And you wonder why I shake you by the shoulder;
Drowsy, you mumble and sigh and turn your head . . .
You are too young to fall asleep for ever;
And when you sleep you remind me of the dead.

SIEGFRIED SASSOON

THE DEATH-BED

He drowsed and was aware of silence heaped
Round him, unshaken as the steadfast walls;
Aqueous-like floating rays of amber light,
Soaring and quivering in the wings of sleep,
Silence and safety; and his mortal shore
Lipped by the inward, moonless waves of death.

Some one was holding water to his mouth.
He swallowed, unresisting; moaned and dropped
Through crimson gloom to darkness; and forgot
The opiate throb and ache that was his wound.
Water—calm, sliding green above the weir;
Water—a sky-lit alley for his boat,
Bird-voiced, and bordered with reflected flowers
And shaken hues of summer; drifting down,
He dipped contented oars, and sighed, and slept.

Night, with a gust of wind, was in the ward,
Blowing the curtain to a glimmering curve.
Night. He was blind; he could not see the stars
Glinting among the wraiths of wandering cloud;
Queer blots of colour, purple, scarlet, green,
Flickered and faded in his drowning eyes.

Rain; he could hear it rustling through the dark;
Fragrance and passionless music woven as one;
Warm rain on drooping roses; pattering showers
That soak the woods; not the harsh rain that sweeps

Behind the thunder, but a trickling peace
Gently and slowly washing life away.

. . . . .

He stirred, shifting his body ; then the pain
Leaped like a prowling beast, and gripped and tore
His groping dreams with grinding claws and fangs.
But some one was beside him ; soon he lay
Shuddering because the evil thing had passed.
And Death, who'd stepped toward him, paused and stared.

Light many lamps and gather round his bed.
Lend him your eyes, warm blood, and will to live.
Speak to him ; rouse him ; you may save him yet.
He's young ; he hated war ; how should he die
When cruel old campaigners win safe through ?

But Death replied : " I choose him." So he went,
And there was silence in the summer night ;
Silence and safety ; and the veils of sleep.
Then, far away, the thudding of the guns.

SIEGFRIED SASSOON

ANTHEM FOR DOOMED YOUTH

What passing-bells for these who die as cattle ?
  Only the monstrous anger of the guns.
Only the stuttering rifles' rapid rattle
  Can patter out their hasty orisons.
No mockeries for them from prayers or bells,
  Nor any voice of mourning save the choirs,—
The shrill, demented choirs of wailing shells ;
  And bugles calling for them from sad shires.

What candles may be held to speed them all ?
  Not in the hands of boys, but in their eyes
  Shall shine the holy glimmers of good-byes.
The pallor of girls' brows shall be their pall ;
Their flowers the tenderness of silent minds,
And each slow dusk a drawing-down of blinds.

WILFRED OWEN

FRAGMENT: THE ABYSS OF WAR

As bronze may be much beautified
By lying in the dark damp soil,
So men who fade in dust of warfare fade
Fairer, and sorrow blooms their soul.

Like pearls which noble women wear
And, tarnishing, awhile confide
Unto the old salt sea to feed,
Many return more lustrous than they were.

WILFRED OWEN

STRANGE MEETING

It seemed that out of battle I escaped
Down some profound dull tunnel, long since scooped
Through granites which titanic wars had groined.
Yet also there encumbered sleepers groaned,
Too fast in thought or death to be bestirred.
Then, as I probed them, one sprang up, and stared
With piteous recognition in fixed eyes,
Lifting distressful hands as if to bless.
And by his smile, I knew that sullen hall,
By his dead smile I knew we stood in Hell.
With a thousand pains that vision's face was grained;
Yet no blood reached there from the upper ground,
And no guns thumped, or down the flues made moan.
'Strange friend,' I said, 'here is no cause to mourn.'
'None,' said the other, 'save the undone years,
The hopelessness. Whatever hope is yours,
Was my life also; I went hunting wild
After the wildest beauty in the world,
Which lies not calm in eyes, or braided hair,
But mocks the steady running of the hour,

And if it grieves, grieves richlier than here.
For by my glee might many men have laughed,
And of my weeping something had been left,
Which must die now. I mean the truth untold,
The pity of war, the pity war distilled.
Now men will go content with what we spoiled.
Or, discontent, boil bloody, and be spilled.
They will be swift with swiftness of the tigress,
None will break ranks, though nations trek from progress.
Courage was mine, and I had mystery,
Wisdom was mine, and I had mastery ;
To miss the march of this retreating world
Into vain citadels that are not walled.
Then, when much blood had clogged their chariot-wheels
I would go up and wash them from sweet wells,
Even with truths that lie too deep for taint.
I would have poured my spirit without stint
But not through wounds ; not on the cess of war.
Foreheads of men have bled where no wounds were.
I am the enemy you killed, my friend.
I knew you in this dark ; for so you frowned
Yesterday through me as you jabbed and killed.
I parried ; but my hands were loath and cold.
Let us sleep now . . .'

WILFRED OWEN

LIGHTS OUT

I have come to the borders of sleep,
The unfathomable deep
Forest where all must lose
Their way, however straight
Or winding, soon or late ;
They cannot choose.

Many a road and track
That, since the dawn's first crack,
Up to the forest brink,
Deceived the travellers,
Suddenly now blurs,
And in they sink.

Here love ends,
Despair, ambition ends ;
All pleasure and all trouble,
Although most sweet or bitter,
Here ends in sleep that is sweeter
Than tasks most noble.

There is not any book
Or face of dearest look
That I would not turn from now
To go into the unknown
I must enter, and leave, alone,
I know not how.

The tall forest towers ;
Its cloudy foliage lowers
Ahead, shelf above shelf ;
Its silence I hear and obey
That I may lose my way
And myself.

EDWARD THOMAS

DIFFUGERE NIVES, 1917

TO J. C. S.

The snows have fled, the hail, the lashing rain,
Before the spring.
The grass is starred with buttercups again,
The blackbirds sing.

Now spreads the month that feast of lovely things
We loved of old.
Once more the swallow glides with darkling wings
Against the gold.

Now the brown bees about the peach trees boom
Upon the walls;
And far away beyond the orchard's bloom
The cuckoo calls.

The season holds a festival of light
For you, for me;
But shadows are abroad, there falls a blight
On each green tree.

And every leaf unfolding, every flower
Brings bitter meed;
Beauty of the morning and the evening hour
Quickens our need.

All is reborn, but never any spring
Can bring back this;
Nor any fullness of midsummer bring
The voice we miss.

The smiling eyes shall smile on us no more;
The laughter clear,
Too far away on the forbidden shore,
We shall not hear.

Bereft of these until the day we die
We both must dwell;
Alone, alone, and haunted by the cry:
'Hail and farewell!'

Yet when the scythe of Death shall near us hiss
Through the cold air,
Then on the shuddering marge of the abyss
They will be there.

They will be there to lift us from sheer space
And empty night;
And we shall turn and see them face to face
In the new light.

So shall we pay the unabated price
Of their release,
And found on our consenting sacrifice
Their lasting peace.

The hopes that fall like leaves before the wind,
The baffling waste,
And every earthly joy that leaves behind
A mortal taste.

The uncompleted end of all things dear,
The clanging door
Of death, for ever loud with the last fear,
Haunt them no more.

Without them the awakening world is dark
With dust and mire;
Yet as they went they flung to us a spark,
A thread of fire.

To guide us while beneath the sombre skies
Faltering we tread,
Until for us like morning stars shall rise
The deathless dead.

MAURICE BARING

RAIN

Rain, midnight rain, nothing but the wild rain
On this bleak hut, and solitude, and me
Remembering again that I shall die
And neither hear the rain nor give it thanks
For washing me cleaner than I have been
Since I was born into this solitude.
Blessed are the dead that the rain rains upon :
But here I pray that none whom once I loved
Is dying to-night, or lying still awake
Solitary, listening to the rain,
Either in pain or thus in sympathy
Helpless among the living and the dead,
Like a cold water among broken reeds,
Myriads of broken reeds all still and stiff,
Like me who have no love which this wild rain
Has not dissolved except the love of death.
If love it be for what is perfect and
Cannot, the tempest tells me, disappoint.

EDWARD THOMAS

STANZAS FROM 'ELEGY FOR EDWARD THOMAS'

The clods of battlefields are red
With immortality : the dead
In their magnificence arise
To shine before us through the skies.

And miracles of heavenly mirth
In all the trees and plants on earth
Rebuke from every flower and leaf
Man's vain impertinence of grief.

And feathered birds, and fishes finned,
And clouds and rain and calm and wind,
And sun and moon and stars, declare
All life is one life, everywhere ;

That nothing dies to die for good
In clay or dust, in stone or wood,
But only rests awhile, to keep
Life's ancient covenant with Sleep.

CHARLES DALMON

THE CHIEF CENTURIONS

(FROM 'THE TRAGEDY OF POMPEY THE GREAT')

Man is a sacred city, built of marvellous earth.
Life was lived nobly here to give this body birth.
Something was in this brain and in this eager hand.
Death is so dumb and blind, Death cannot understand.
Death drifts the brain with dust and soils the young limbs' glory.
Death makes women a dream and men a traveller's story,
Death drives the lovely soul to wander under the sky,
Death opens unknown doors. It is most grand to die.

JOHN MASEFIELD

THE PURIFICATION

They have gone over, the god, the friend, the lover,
They have gone over.
It is growing grey now;
There comes the end of day now.

They were signs then, the stars were a glory for men,
They were signs then.
Those lights flare unseen now,
Things paltry and mean now.

They were true pleasure, the friendly trust, the praise without measure,
They were true pleasure.
Praise is an empty sound now.
Trust treads no firm ground now.

They were music, joy, and truth, the kisses she gave him in youth,
They were music, joy, and truth.
They are less beautiful now;
They are but dutiful now.

Aye, they have come to an end, the god, the lover, the friend;
They have come to an end.
The soul is alone now;
Strong, naked, full-grown now.

RICHARD CHURCH

THE DEAD

These hearts were woven of human joys and cares,
  Washed marvellously with sorrow, swift to mirth.
The years had given them kindness. Dawn was theirs,
  And sunset, and the colours of the earth.
These had seen movement, and heard music; known
  Slumber and waking; loved; gone proudly friended;
Felt the quick stir of wonder; sat alone;
  Touched flowers and furs and cheeks. All this is ended.

There are waters blown by changing winds to laughter
And lit by the rich skies, all day. And after,
Frost, with a gesture, stays the waves that dance
  And wandering loveliness. He leaves a white
Unbroken glory, a gathered radiance,
  A width, a shining peace, under the night.

RUPERT BROOKE

OUR FRIENDS GO WITH US

Our friends go with us as we go
  Down the long path where Beauty wends,
Where all we love forgathers, so
  Why should we fear to join our friends?

Who would survive them to outlast
  His children; to outwear his fame—
Left when the Triumph has gone past—
  To win from Age, not Time, a name?

Then do not shudder at the knife
  That Death's indifferent hand drives home,
But with the Strivers leave the Strife
  Nor, after Cæsar, skulk in Rome.

OLIVER ST. JOHN GOGARTY

FOR THE FALLEN

With proud thanksgiving, a mother for her children,
England mourns for her dead across the sea.
Flesh of her flesh they were, spirit of her spirit,
Fallen in the cause of the free.

Solemn the drums thrill : Death august and royal
Sings sorrow up into immortal spheres.
There is music in the midst of desolation
And glory that shines upon our tears.

They went with songs to the battle, they were young,
Straight of limb, true of eye, steady and aglow,
They were staunch to the end against odds uncounted,
They fell with their faces to the foe.

They shall grow not old, as we that are left grow old :
Age shall not weary them, nor the years condemn.
At the going down of the sun and in the morning
We will remember them.

They mingle not with their laughing comrades again ;
They sit no more at familiar tables of home ;
They have no lot in our labour of the day-time ;
They sleep beyond England's foam.

But where our desires are and our hopes profound,
Felt as a well-spring that is hidden from sight,
To the innermost heart of their own land they are known
As the stars are known to the Night ;

As the stars that shall be bright when we are dust,
Moving in marches upon the heavenly plain,
As the stars that are starry in the time of our darkness,
To the end, to the end they remain.

LAURENCE BINYON

III

1918–1930

THE RIDGE: 1919

Here on the ridge where the shrill north-easter trails
Low clouds along the snow,
And in a streaming moonlit vapour veils
The peopled earth below,

Let me, O life, a little while forget
The horror of past years—
Man and his agony and bloody sweat,
The terror and the tears,

And struggle only with the mist and snow
Against the hateless wind,
Till scourged and shriven I again may go
To dwell among my kind.

WILFRID GIBSON

IN WILTSHIRE

Fairest of valleys, in this full-bloomed night,
  Whose air so lullingly,
  Whose dusk so understandingly
Embraces us, and gives us more than light,

O happy valley, with your poplars manned
  Beneath the visiting moon,
  And talking to the loitering moon,
Vast as desire, and by an owl-call spanned,

Perfection is your name; yet (foolish prayer!)
  Well would it be for some,
  And safer your dim grace for some,
If nothing in your presence could compare

With a far place. That shuttered lampless mill,
  Those white-glanced pools are like,
  These tangled cliffs are all too like
A valley where our dream-selves tremble still.

The wires and poles that cut the ridge and sky,
  The blackness of these groves,
  The secret patter of river-groves,
These fits and starts of sound, identify.

My feet along this road, above that stream
  Drop into marching-time,
  Make wild arithmetic of time—
So like this valley and that dead one seem.

EDMUND BLUNDEN

HUNGER

I come among the peoples like a shadow.
I sit down by each man's side.

None sees me, but they look on one another,
And know that I am there.

My silence is like the silence of the tide
That buries the playground of children;

Like the deepening of frost in the slow night,
When birds are dead in the morning.

Armies trample, invade, destroy,
With guns roaring from earth and air.

I am more terrible than armies,
I am more feared than cannon.

Kings and chancellors give commands;
I give no command to any;

But I am listened to more than kings
And more than passionate orators.

I unswear words, and undo deeds.
Naked things know me.

I am first and last to be felt of the living.
I am Hunger.

LAURENCE BINYON

THE DANCER

The young girl dancing lifts her face,
  Passive among the drooping flowers ;
The jazz band clatters sticks and bones
  In a bright rhythm through the hours.

The men in black conduct her round ;
  With small sensations they are blind :
Thus Saturn's Moons revolve embraced
  And through the cosmos wind.

But Saturn has not that strange look
  Unhappy, still, and far away,
As though upon the face of Night
  Lay the bright wreck of day.

W. J. TURNER

OLD SOLDIER

We wander now who marched before,
Hawking our bran from door to door,
While other men from the mill take their flour :
  So it is to be an Old Soldier.

Old, bare and sore, we look on the hound
Turning upon the stiff frozen ground,
Nosing the mould, with the night around :
  So it is to be an Old Soldier.

And we who once rang out like a bell,
Have nothing now to show or to sell ;
Old bones to carry, old stories to tell :
  So it is to be an Old Soldier.

PADRAIC COLUM

REPORT ON EXPERIENCE

I have been young, and now am not too old ;
And I have seen the righteous forsaken,
His health, his honour and his quality taken.
This is not what we were formerly told.

I have seen a green country, useful to the race,
Knocked silly with guns and mines, its villages vanished,
Even the last rat and last kestrel banished—
God bless us all, this was peculiar grace.

I knew Seraphina ; Nature gave her hue
Glance, sympathy, note, like one from Eden.
I saw her smile warp, heard her lyric deaden ;
She turned to harlotry ;—this I took to be new.

Say what you will, our God sees how they run.
These disillusions are His curious proving
That He loves humanity and will go on loving ;
Over there are faith, life, virtue in the sun.

EDMUND BLUNDEN

A THOUGHT

When I look into a glass,
Myself's my only care,
But I look into a pool
For all the wonders there.

When I look into a glass
I see a fool :
But I see a wise man
When I look into a pool.

W. H. DAVIES

WEATHERS

This is the weather the cuckoo likes,
And so do I ;
When showers betumble the chestnut spikes,
And nestlings fly :
And the little brown nightingale bills his best,
And they sit outside at 'The Travellers' Rest,'
And maids come forth sprig-muslin drest,
And citizens dream of the south and west,
And so do I.

This is the weather the shepherd shuns,
And so do I ;
When beeches drip in browns and duns,
And thresh, and ply ;
And hill-hid tides throb, throe on throe,
And meadow rivulets overflow,
And drops on gate-bars hang in a row,
And rooks in families homeward go,
And so do I.

THOMAS HARDY

IN THE FIELDS

Lord, when I look at lovely things which pass,
  Under old trees the shadows of young leaves
Dancing to please the wind along the grass,
  Or the gold stillness of the August sun on the August
        sheaves;
Can I believe there is a heavenlier world than this?
    And if there is
Will the strange heart of any everlasting thing
  Bring me these dreams that take my breath away?
They come at evening with the home-flying rooks and the
        scent of hay,
  Over the fields. They come in Spring.

CHARLOTTE MEW

THE VOICE

The sun has turned the dusky hill
  Unto his angry mood; and down
The birchen tops the slant beams spill,
  And light the green and gild the brown;
And the far frontiers of the fern
  Like flame-edged clouds of purple burn.

Great flies boom past and grey moths drowse;
  On spectral leaves plucked fibre-bare
The silkworms drop from hazel boughs,
  Or swing suspended in the air;
The air that throbs, the air that reels,
  While the shrill gnat in madness wheels.

'Cuckoo, Cuckoo!' up the purple vale,
  And 'Itys, Itys!' in the grove;
The slug that creeps across the trail
  Has some hushed trumpet-note of love;
Deep in the wood a girl-voice rings,
  And 'Follow, Follow, Follow!' sings.

RICHARD MANSFIELD

THE BUZZARDS

When evening came and the warm glow grew deeper,
And every tree that bordered the green meadows
And in the yellow cornfields every reaper
And every corn-shock stood above their shadows
Flung eastward from their feet in longer measure,
Serenely far there swam in the sunny height
A buzzard and his mate who took their pleasure
Swirling and poising idly in golden light.

On great pied motionless moth-wings borne along,
So effortless and so strong,
Cutting each other's paths together they glided,
Then wheeled asunder till they soared divided
Two valleys' width (as though it were delight
To part like this, being sure they could unite
So swiftly in their empty, free dominion),
Curved headlong downward, towered up the sunny steep,
Then, with a sudden lift of the one great pinion,
Swung proudly to a curve, and from its height
Took half a mile of sunlight in one long sweep.

And we, so small on the swift immense hillside,
Stood tranced until our souls arose uplifted
On those far-sweeping, wide,
Strong curves of flight—swayed up and hugely drifted,
Were washed, made strong and beautiful in the tide
Of sun-bathed air. But far beneath, beholden
Through shining deeps of air, the fields were golden,
And rosy burned the heather where cornfields ended.

And still those buzzards whirled, while light withdrew
Out of the vales and to surging slopes ascended,
Till the loftiest flaming died to blue.

MARTIN ARMSTRONG

THREE NOCTURNS

I

The valleys that we knew in sunlit hours
Are vast and vague as seas ;
Wan as the blackthorn flowers
That quiver in the first spring-scented breeze ;
Far as the frosted hollows of the moon.

The sighing woods are still
That climb this mouse-soft hill,
Tall nettles rank with rain
Scent all the woods with some ancestral fear.

Trees rustle by the water—soon
A voice sings near,
Too loud, to ward off fright :
Then fainter, and in vain,
Sings in the yielding and unechoing night.

II

An owl, horned wizard of the night,
Flaps through the air, so soft and still ;
Moans, as it wings its flight
Toward the mist-wrapped hill.

III

The milky clouds, dispersing, drift away,
Splashing the woods with patches of pale light,
Sail high above like silver ships, display
The dazzling myriad blossoms of the night.

Ah ! It is worth full many a sun-gilt hour
To see the heavens bursting into flower.

OSBERT SITWELL

THE SWANS

How lovely are these swans,
That float like high proud galleons
Cool in the summer heat,
And waving leaf-like feet
Divide with narrow breasts of snow
In a smooth surge
This water that is mostly sky;
So lovely that I know
Death cannot kill such birds,
It could but wound them, mortally.

ANDREW YOUNG

THE BIRD

The blackbird darted through the boughs
Trailing his whistle in a shrill dispute,
'Why do you loiter near our house?'
But I was mute.
Though as he perched with sidelong head
I might have said,
'I never notice nests or lovers
In hedges or in covers;
I have enough to do
In my own way to be unnoticed too.'

ANDREW YOUNG

A BIRD'S EPITAPH

Here lies a little bird,
Once all day long
Through Martha's house was heard
His rippling song.

Tread lightly where he lies
Beneath this stone
With nerveless wings, closed eyes,
And sweet voice gone.

MARTIN ARMSTRONG

THE CHALK-CLIFF

Blasted and bored and undermined
  By quarrying seas
Reared the erect chalk-cliff with black flints lined.
  (Flints drop like nuts from trees
When the frost bites
The chalk on winter nights.)

Save for frail shade of jackdaw's flight
  No night was there,
But blue-skyed summer and a cliff so white
  It stood like frozen air;
Foot slipped on damp
Chalk where the limpets camp.

With only purple of sea-stock
  And jackdaw's shade
To mitigate that blazing height of chalk
  I stood like a soul strayed
In paradise
Hiding my blinded eyes.

ANDREW YOUNG

BOATS AT NIGHT

How lovely is the sound of oars at night
  And unknown voices, borne through windless air,
From shadowy vessels floating out of sight
  Beyond the harbour lantern's broken glare
To those piled rocks that make on the dark wave
  Only a darker stain. The splashing oars
Slide softly on as in an echoing cave
  And with the whisper of the unseen shores
Mingle their music, till the bell of night
  Murmurs reverberations low and deep
That droop towards the land in swooning flight
  Like whispers from the lazy lips of sleep.
The oars grow faint. Below the cloud-dim hill
The shadows fade and now the bay is still.

EDWARD SHANKS

THE RUINED CHAPEL

From meadows with the sheep so shorn
They, not their lambs, seem newly born,
Through the graveyard I pass,
Where only blue plume-thistle waves
And headstones lie so deep in grass
They follow dead men to their graves ;
And as I enter by no door
This chapel where the slow moss crawls,
I wonder that so small a floor
Can have the sky for roof, mountains for walls.

ANDREW YOUNG

THE VILLAIN

While joy gave clouds the light of stars,
  That beamed where'er they looked ;
And calves and lambs had tottering knees,
  Excited while they sucked ;
While every bird enjoyed his song,
Without one thought of harm or wrong—
I turned my head and saw the wind,
  Not far from where I stood,
Dragging the corn by her golden hair,
  Into a dark and lonely wood.

W. H. DAVIES

THE SECRET WOOD

Where there is nothing more to see
Than this old earth-bound tree
That years ago dry sawdust bled
But sprouts each spring a leaf or two
As though it tried not to be dead,
Or that down-hanging broken bough
That keeps its withered leaves till now
Like a dead man that cannot move
Or take his clothes off,
What is it that I seek or who,
Fearing from passer-by
Intrusion of a foot or eye?
I only know
Though all men of earth's beauty speak
Beauty here I do not seek
More than I sought it on my mother's cheek.

ANDREW YOUNG

WINTER THE HUNTSMAN

Through his iron glades
Rides Winter the Huntsman.
All colour fades
As his horn is heard sighing.

Far through the forest
His wild hooves crash and thunder
Till many a mighty branch
Is torn asunder.

And the red reynard creeps
To his hole near the river,
The copper leaves fall
And the bare trees shiver

As night creeps from the ground,
Hides each tree from its brother,
And each dying sound
Reveals yet another.

Is it Winter the Huntsman
Who gallops through his iron glades,
Cracking his cruel whip
To the gathering shades?

OSBERT SITWELL

LAST SNOW

Although the snow still lingers
Heaped on the ivy's blunt webbed fingers
And painting tree-trunks on one side,
Here in this sunlit ride
The fresh unchristened things appear,
Leaf, spathe and stem,
With crumbs of earth clinging to them
To show the way they came,
But no flower yet to tell their name,
And one green spear
Stabbing a dead leaf from below
Kills winter at a blow.

ANDREW YOUNG

THE SEED SHOP

Here in a quiet and dusty room they lie,
Faded as crumbled stone or shifting sand,
Forlorn as ashes, shrivelled, scentless, dry—
Meadows and gardens running through my hand.

In this brown husk a dale of hawthorn dreams,
A cedar in this narrow cell is thrust;
It will drink deeply of a century's streams,
These lilies shall make summer on my dust.

Here in their safe and simple house of death,
Sealed in their shells a million roses leap;
Here I can blow a garden with my breath,
And in my hand a forest lies asleep.

MURIEL STUART

TRUE LOVE

Like as herb and tree in May
  Flourish from the root,
Every lusty heart must rise,
And start to love, and fare likewise,—
  Flower first, then fruit.

For he giveth courage then
  That lusty month of May,—
He calls to mind what true love is,
Old service and old gentleness,
  Forgot upon the way.

For, know you, never worshipful
  Man nor woman neither
But each loved the other well,
More than anyone can tell,
  Each one loving either.

Such love I call virtuous love ;
  But men, nowadays
Cannot love,—not seven night,
But they must have all love's delight,
  Fruit and grace.

Hasty heart,—it cooleth soon,
  All its love soon told :
Winter rasure soon doth rase
Summer ;—so is love these days,
  Soon hot, soon cold !

This is no stability :
  The old love was not so :
Men would love for seven year,
In loving truth and tender fear,
  And wantonness not know.

Call to your remembrance then,
  The joyous month of May,
And call up True Love to you here,
Who while she loves, loves very dear,
  And loves the same alway.

ERNEST RHYS

AFTER LONG SILENCE

Speech after long silence ; it is right,
All other lovers being estranged or dead,
Unfriendly lamplight hid under its shade,
The curtains drawn upon unfriendly night,
That we descant and yet again descant
Upon the supreme theme of Art and Song :
Bodily decrepitude is wisdom ; young
We loved each other and were ignorant.

W. B. YEATS

LOST LOVE

His eyes are quickened so with grief,
He can watch a grass or leaf
Every instant grow ; he can
Clearly through a flint wall see,
Or watch the startled spirit flee
From the throat of a dead man.
Across two counties he can hear
And catch your words before you speak.
The woodlouse or the maggot's weak
Clamour rings in his sad ear,
And noise so slight it would surpass
Credence—drinking sound of grass,
Worm talk, clashing jaws of moth
Chumbling holes in cloth ;
The groans of ants who undertake
Gigantic loads for honour's sake
(Their sinews creak, their breath comes thin) ;
Whir of spiders when they spin,
And minute whispering, mumbling, sighs
Of idle grubs and flies.
This man is quickened so with grief,
He wanders god-like or like thief
Inside and out, below, above,
Without relief seeking lost love.

ROBERT GRAVES

I SPEND MY DAYS VAINLY

I spend my days vainly,
  Not in delight;
Though the world is elate,
  And tastes her joys finely.

Here wrapped in slow musing
  Lies my dark mind,
To no music attuned
  Save its own, and despising

The lark for remoteness,
  The thrush for bold lying,
The soft wind for blowing,
  And the round sun for brightness.

O tarry for me, sweet;
  I shall stir, I shall wake!
And the melody you seek
  Shall be lovely, though late.

FRANK KENDON

BY THE WEIR

A scent of espatto grass—and again I recall
That hour we spent by the weir of the paper-mill,
Watching together the curving thunderous fall
Of frothing amber, bemused by the roar until
My mind was as blank as the speckless sheets that wound
On the hot steel ironing rollers perpetually turning
In the humming dark rooms of the mill—all sense discerning
By the stunning and dazzling oblivion of hill-waters drowned.

And my heart was empty of memory, hope, and desire
Till, rousing, I looked afresh on your face as you gazed—
Behind you an old gnarled fruit-tree in one still fire
Of innumerable flame in the sun of October blazed,
Scarlet and gold that the first white frost would spill
With eddying flicker and patter of dead leaves falling—
I looked on your face as an outcast from Eden recalling
A vision of Eve as she dallied bewildered and still

By the serpent-encircled Tree of Knowledge that flamed
With gold and scarlet of good and evil, her eyes
Rapt on the river of life: then bright and untamed
By the labour and sorrow and fear of a world that dies,
Your ignorant eyes looked up into mine; and I knew
That never our hearts should be one till your young lips had
tasted
The core of the bitter-sweet fruit, and, wise and toil-wasted,
You should stand at my shoulder an outcast from Eden too.

WILFRID GIBSON

ABÉLARD TELLS HIS LOVE TO HÉLOÏSE

Art thou not lovely?
Say yes, say yes, and doubt not,
Say . . .
What dost thou say?
But to me thou art full lovely,
So that I love thee
And would heal me
At thy fair fountain.

For thou art strength to me
And length of days
In life that is shortened,
Bright threads of light
In the dusk's haze.

Swing to! Swing to!
Swing shutters upon the night
That the light may here reign.

Such kindness thine eyes spray
Clear sight in my blindness,
Thou cleanser of pain!

For when I am with thee
What is death or ambition?
In the scent of thy being
All darkness is slain.

HERBERT PALMER

LOVE'S FRAGILITY

Hard above all things mortal is
To sacrifice our love's return:
We shudder and are bare of bliss
And our hearts mourn.

For love is lighter than men say;
None has been known as light as he.
His whole profundity is play,
Pleasant to see.

He's born in the unspoken word
Or the quick intercourse of eyes.
A touch, and all his power is stirred;
He sings, he flies.

He veers and trembles at a breath,
As mutable as thistle-down.
He faints, and he is sick to death
For a mere frown.

Some bring report of other lands
Where love's fragility is strong.
They compass him with iron bands;
He suffers long.

They cast him in a dungeon-keep;
He digs and burrows like a mole;
For forty days denying sleep,
Yet issues whole.

I well believe that love is strong
To bear the heaviest dint of doom;
Confronts the tempest with a song;
Conquers the tomb.

I well believe that love is firm
When love is fostered between two :
Mortality can set no term
    If both be true.

But oh, how weak the love of one
If counterchange of love's forbad ;
If love is plaintive and alone
    And poor and sad.

The mouth is filled with bitterness ;
The echoing air is cold with scorn.
We shudder and are bare of bliss
    And our hearts mourn.

ALAN PORTER

SICK LOVE

O Love, be fed with apples while you may,
And feel the sun and go in royal array,
A smiling innocent on the heavenly causeway,

Though in what listening horror for the cry
That soars in outer blackness dismally,
The dumb blind beast, the paranoiac fury :

Be warm, enjoy the season, lift your head,
Exquisite in the pulse of tainted blood,
That infirm passion not to be despised.

Take your delight in momentariness,
Walk between dark and dark—a shining space
With the grave's narrowness, though not its peace.

ROBERT GRAVES

WHEN THE ECSTATIC BODY GRIPS

When the ecstatic body grips
Its heaven, with little sobbing cries,
And lips are crushed on hot blind lips,
I read strange pity in your eyes.

For that in you which is not mine,
And that in you which I love best,
And that, which my day-thoughts divine
Masterless still, still unpossessed,

Sits in the blue eyes' frightened stare,
A naked lonely-dwelling thing,
A frail thing from its body-lair
Drawn at my body's summoning;

Whispering low, ' O unknown man,
Whose hunger on my hunger wrought,
Body shall give what body can,
Shall give you all—save what you sought.'

Whispering, ' O secret one, forgive,
Forgive and be content though still
Beyond the blood's surrender live
The darkness of the separate will.

' Enough if in the veins we know
Body's delirium, body's peace—
Ask not that ghost to ghost shall go,
Essence in essence merge and cease.'

But swiftly, as in sudden sleep,
That You in you is veiled or dead;
And the world's shrunken to a heap
Of hot flesh straining on a bed.

E. R. DODDS

AN UNMARRIED MOTHER SINGS

Lull, lullaby, all is still and the sea lakes are
Stretching the light of daytime towards the first star—
Stretching the grey light on me; and your child at rest,
Snuggling the flush of sleep on my troubled breast.

You, gentle love, I would rather have here at ease;
You, whose strong love did anoint my limbs with peace;
You, O outlawed love, not a priest, not a ghostly thief
Dare take you now from my thought that's lockjawed by grief.

What peace of mind can you have, love? Ah why not go,
Wear down your spade to the butt till sweat quenches your woe,
Yes, wear down your black grief, like many a love-crazed man
Who wrenches grass out of his pain in some barren glen.

Go where you will, sacred life, you're my very own;
My breath, my breasts, they are full of you, you alone;
So, marked till death with your likeness my starved womb groans,
Since you're nailed in love onto my four bones . . .

Lull, lullaby, lullaby, lulla, lullaby.

F. R. HIGGINS

LULLABY

Beloved, may your sleep be sound
That have found it where you fed.
What were all the world's alarms
To mighty Paris when he found
Sleep upon a golden bed
That first dawn in Helen's arms?

Sleep, beloved, such a sleep
As did that wild Tristram know
When, the potion's work being done,
Roe could run or doe could leap
Under oak and beechen bough,
Roe could leap or doe could run;

Such a sleep and sound as fell
Upon Eurotas' grassy bank
When the holy bird, that there
Accomplished his predestined will,
From the limbs of Leda sank
But not from her protecting care.

W. B. YEATS

AURELIA

When within my arms I hold you,
Motionless in long surrender,
Then what love-words can I summon,
Tender as my heart is tender?

When within your arms you hold me,
And kisses speak your love unspoken,
Then my eyes with tears run over,
And my very heart is broken.

ROBERT NICHOLS

FREEDOM

Now heaven be thanked, I am out of love again!
I have been long a slave, and now am free;
I have been tortured, and am eased of pain;
I have been blind, and now my eyes can see;
I have been lost, and now my way lies plain;
I have been caged, and now I hold the key;
I have been mad, and now at last am sane;
I am wholly I that was but half of me.
  So a free man, my dull proud path I plod,
  Who, tortured, blind, mad, caged, was once a God.

JAN STRUTHER

FROM 'THEME WITH VARIATIONS'

No pride hath he who sings of escape from love:
All songs of escape from love are songs of despair:
Who so hath gat him away hath got nowhere.

He sings below all that he knows as above:
He hath no mind for the gentle, heart for the fair:

No pride hath he who sings of escape from love:
All songs of escape from love are songs of despair.

Who doth not sing as the wild-dove sings to the dove,
The night-wild sprite to the moon, of love is bare:
He knows not pity, passion, praise, nor prayer:

No pride hath he who sings of escape from love:
All songs of escape from love are songs of despair:
Who so hath gat him away hath got nowhere.

JAMES STEPHENS

THE BEAUTIFUL

Three things there are more beautiful
Than any man could wish to see:
The first, it is a full-rigged ship
Sailing with all her sails set free;
The second, when the wind and sun
Are playing in a field of corn;
The third, a woman, young and fair,
Showing her child before it is born.

W. H. DAVIES

TOM'S ANGEL

No one was in the fields
But me and Polly Flint,
When, like a giant across the grass,
The flaming angel went.

It was budding time in May,
And green as green could be,
And all in his height he went along
Past Polly Flint and me.

We'd been playing in the woods,
And Polly up, and ran,
And hid her face, and said,
'Tom! Tom! The Man! The Man!'

And I upturned; and there,
Like flames across the sky,
With wings all bristling, came
The Angel striding by.

And a chaffinch overhead
Kept whistling in the tree
While the Angel, blue as fire, came on
Past Polly Flint and me.

And I saw his hair, and all
The ruffling of his hem,
As over the clovers his bare feet
Trod without stirring them.

Polly—she cried; and, oh!
We ran, until the lane
Turned by the miller's roaring wheel,
And we were safe again.

WALTER DE LA MARE

THE SPRIG OF LIME

He lay, and those who watched him were amazed
To see unheralded beneath the lids
Twin tears, new-gathered at the price of pain,
Start and at once run crookedly athwart
Cheeks channelled long by pain, never by tears.
So desolate, too, the sigh next uttered
They had wept also, but his great lips moved,
And bending down one heard, ' A sprig of lime ;
Bring me a sprig of lime.' Whereat she stole
With dumb sign forth to pluck the thing he craved.

So lay he till a lime-twig had been snapped
From some still branch that swept the outer grass
Far from the silver pillar of the bole,
Which, mounting past the house's crusted roof,
Split into massy limbs, crossed boughs, a maze
Of close-compacted intercontorted staffs
Bowered in foliage, wherethrough the sun
Shot sudden showers of light or crystal spars
Or wavered in a green and vitreous flood.

And all the while in faint and fainter tones,
Scarce audible on deepened evening's hush,
He framed his curious and last request
For ' lime, a sprig of lime.' Her trembling hand
Closed his loose fingers on the awkward stem,
Covered about with gentle heart-shaped leaves
And under dangling, pale as honey-wax,
Square clusters of sweet-scented starry flowers.
She laid his bent arm back upon his breast,
Then watched above white knuckles clenched in prayer.
He never moved. Only at last his eyes
Opened, then brightened in such avid gaze
She feared the coma mastered him again. . . .
But no ; strange sobs rose chuckling in his throat,
A stranger ecstasy suffused the flesh
Of that just mask so sun-dried, gouged and old,
Which few—too few !—had loved, too many feared.
' Father ! ' she cried ; ' Father ! '
He did not hear.

She knelt, and, kneeling, drank the scent of limes,
Blown round the slow blind by a vesperal gust,
Till the room swam. So the lime-incense blew
Into her life as once it had in his,
Though how and when and with what ageless charge
Of sorrow and deep joy how could she know?

Sweet lime so hushèdly at the height of noon
Diffusing dizzy fragrance from your boughs,
Tasselled with blossoms more innumerable
Than the black bees, the uproar of whose toil
Fills your green vaults, winning such metheglin
As clouds their sappy cells, distil, as once
Ye used, your sunniest emanations
Towards the window where a woman kneels—
She who within that room in childish hours
Lay through the lasting murmur of blanch'd noon
Behind the sultry blind, now full, now flat,
Drinking anew of every odorous breath,
Supremely happy in her ignorance
Of Time that hastens hourly and of Death
Who need not haste. Scatter your fumes, O lime,
Loose from each hispid star of citron bloom,
Tangled beneath the labyrinthine boughs,
Cloud on such stinging cloud of exhalation
As reeks of youth, fierce life, and summer's prime,
Though hardly now shall he in that dusk room
Savour your sweetness, since the very sprig,
Profuse of blossom and of essences,
He smells not, who in a paltering hand
Clasps it laid close his peaked and gleaming face
Propped in the pillow. Breathe silent, lofty lime,
Your curfew secrets out in fervid scent
To the attendant shadows! Tinge the air
Of the midsummer night that now begins,
At an owl's oaring flight from dusk to dusk,
And downward caper of the giddy bat
Hawking against the lustre of bare skies,
With something of th' unfathomable bliss
He, who lies dying there, knew once of old

In the serene trance of a summer night,
When with th' abundance of his young bride's hair
Loosed on his breast he lay and dared not sleep,
Listening for the scarce motion of your boughs,
Which sighed with bliss as she with blissful sleep,
And drinking desperately each honied wave
Of perfume wafted past the ghostly blind,
First knew th' implacable and bitter sense
Of Time that hastes and Death who need not haste.
Shed your last sweetness, limes!
But now no more.
She, fruit of that night's love, she heeds you not,
Who bent, compassionate, to the dim floor,
Takes up the sprig of lime and presses it
In pain against the stumbling of her heart,
Knowing, untold, he cannot need it now.

ROBERT NICHOLS

DIVORCE

(*To My Father*)

When Love, born first of thought and will,
Ponders what dooms it shall fulfil,
And knows itself and names,
Sole son of man to meet and dare
All lusts couched in the body's lair
Till he their fury tames:

From whom his duty shall he learn,
To whom for admonition turn,
That his young heart may know
What infinite fatality
Life shall wreak on him, nor shall he
Refuse to undergo?

Whom but such souls as, torn with pain,
Have proved all things and proved them vain
And have no joy thereof,
Yet lifting their pale heads august
Declare the frame of things is just,
Nor shall the balance move?

Each to his teachers—nor of mine,
Though long and lofty be the line,
  Shall any, sir, be set
More high in this poor heart than you
Who taught me all the good I knew
  Ere Love and I were met :

Great good and small,—the terms of fate,
The nature of the gods, the strait
  Path of the climbing mind,
The freedom of the commonwealth,
The laws of soul's and body's health,
  The commerce of mankind.

The charges launched on Christendom
You showed me, ere the years had come
  When I endured the strain,
Yet warned me, unfair tales to balk,
What slanders still the pious talk
  Of Voltaire and Tom Paine.

What early verse of mine you chid,
Rebuked the use of *doth* and *did*,
  Measuring the rhythm's beat ;
Or read with me how Cæsar passed,
On the March Ides, to hold his last
  Senate at Pompey's feet !

What words of grace, not understood
Until the years had proved them good,
  Your wisdom set in me,—
Until the asps of blindness lay
Upon your brows and sucked away
  Joy, sweetness, memory.

Now all the pages of the wise,
Whereon for happiness your eyes
  Were wisely apt to pore,
Upon another's mouth depend,
And friend by step is known from friend,
  And faces seen no more.

Now, now the work all men must do
Is mightily begun in you ;
  And the sure-cutting days
Leave you, disfurnished, dispossessed
Of earth, to seek your spirit's rest
  Beyond our mortal ways.

Now, now in you the great divorce
Begins, whose everlasting source
  Sprang up before the sun,
Whose chill dividing waters roll
'Twixt flesh and spirit, mind and soul,—
  Than death more deeply run :

Divorce, sole healer of divorce ;
For our deep sickness of remorse
  Sole draught medicinal,
Which Grief from bitter herbage brews
Where Babylonish waters ooze
  O'er Mansoul's shattered wall ;

Divorce, who cries all mortal banns ;
Chief foreman of the artisans
  Who quarry from Time's pit
New stuff for souls, hewn stone on stone ;
Piercer of hearts, by whom is shown
  Death in death implicit ;

Divorce, itself for God and Lord
By the profounder creeds adored :
  Who in eternity,
A bright proceeding ardour, parts
The filial and paternal hearts,
  And knits the riven Three.

O if in holier hours I meet
Your happier head in Sarras' street,
  When our blind years are done,
What song remains shall run to pay
Its duty, sir, from me that day,
  Your pupil and your son.

CHARLES WILLIAMS

FATHER AND SON

Only last week, walking the hushed fields
Of our most lovely Meath, now thinned by November,
I came to where the road from Laracor leads
To the Boyne river—that seemed more lake than river,
Stretched in uneasy light and stript of reeds.

And walking longside an old weir
Of my people's, where nothing stirs—only the shadowed
Leaden flight of a heron up the lean air—
I went unmanly with grief, knowing how my father,
Happy though captive in years, walked last with me there.

Yes, happy in Meath with me for a day
He walked, taking stock of herds hid in their own breathing ;
And naming colts, gusty as wind, once steered by his hand,
Lightnings winked in the eyes that were half shy in greeting
Old friends—the wild blades, when he gallivanted the land.

For that proud, wayward man now my heart breaks—
Breaks for that man whose mind was a secret eyrie,
Whose kind hand was sole signet of his race,
Who curbed me, scorned my green ways, yet increasingly
    loved me
Till Death drew its grey blind down his face.

And yet I am pleased that even my reckless ways
Are living shades of his rich calms and passions—
Witnesses for him and for those faint namesakes
With whom now he is one, under yew branches,
Yes, one in a graven silence no bird breaks.

F. R. HIGGINS

THE IMMIGRANT

When Ruth was old
She'd take her children's children on her knee.
They never wearied to be told
Tales of her girlhood in a far country.

For though her eyes grew dim,
Men said of her, ' Her heart is always young,'
And Boaz, while she spoke to him,
Loved the faint accent of a foreign tongue.

FRANK KENDON

THE FIELDS ARE FULL

The fields are full of summer still,
And breathe again upon the air
From brown dry side of hedge and hill
More sweetness than the sense can bear.

So some old couple, who in youth
With love were filled and over-full,
And loved with strength and loved with truth,
In heavy age are beautiful.

EDWARD SHANKS

AT THE GRAVE OF HENRY VAUGHAN

Above the voiceful windings of a river
An old green slab of simply graven stone
Shuns notice, overshadowed by a yew.
Here Vaughan lies dead, whose name flows on for ever
Through pastures of the spirit washed with dew
And starlit with eternities unknown.

Here sleeps the Silurist ; the loved physician ;
The face that left no portraiture behind ;
The skull that housed white angels and had vision
Of daybreak through the gateways of the mind.
  Here faith and mercy, wisdom and humility
  (Whose influence shall prevail for evermore)
  Shine. And this lowly grave tells Heaven's tranquillity . . .
  And here stand I, a suppliant at the door.

SIEGFRIED SASSOON

I LOVE THE BEGINNING OF ALL RAIN

All things are best when first begun,
A love that's guessed, a race unrun,
And those bright notes that in the brain
Fall brief, beginning of the rain,
Just two or one
That splash, and to the dust belong,
And might have been a rush of song.

GEOFFREY SCOTT

FULL MOON

A man that I know likes the bare tree best;
And many, a moon that's a silver shaving;
But I, whatsoever is all-expressed,—
Full moon, high summer and cornfields waving.

Everyone praises the opening flower . . .
I praise the woman grown wise and tender,
And him who shows me a hard-won power
Of hand or wit in prolific splendour.

CLIFFORD BAX

ALMSWOMEN

At Quincey's moat the straggling village ends,
And there in the almshouse dwell the dearest friends
Of all the village, two old dames that cling
As close as any true-loves in the spring.
Long, long ago they passed three-score-and-ten,
And in this doll's house lived together then;
All things they have in common being so poor,
And their one fear, Death's shadow at the door.
Each sundown makes them mournful, each sunrise
Brings back the brightness in their failing eyes.

How happy go the rich fair weather days
When on the roadside folk stare in amaze
At such a honeycomb of fruit and flowers
As mellows round their threshold; what long hours

They gloat upon their steepling hollyhocks,
Bee's balsams, feathery southernwood and stocks,
Fiery dragon's-mouths, great mallow leaves
For salves, and lemon-plants in bushy sheaves,
Shagged Esau's-hands with five green finger-tips.
Such sweet old names are ever on their lips.

As pleased as little children where these grow
In cobbled pattens and worn gowns they go,
Proud of their wisdom when on gooseberry shoots
They stick egg shells to fright from coming fruits
The brisk-billed rascals ; scanning still to see
Their neighbour owls saunter from tree to tree,
Or in the hushing half-light mouse the lane
Long-winged and lordly.
But when those hours wane
Indoors they ponder, scared by the harsh storm
Whose pelting saracens on the window swarm,
And listen for the mail to clatter past
And church clock's deep bay withering on the blast ;
They feed the fire that flings its freakish light
On pictured kings and queens grotesquely bright,
Platters and pitchers, faded calendars
And graceful hour-glass trim with lavenders.

Many a time they kiss and cry and pray
That both be summoned in the selfsame day,
And wiseman linnet tinkling in his cage
End too with them the friendship of old age,
And all together leave their treasured room
Some bell-like evening when the May's in bloom.

EDMUND BLUNDEN

MRS. REECE LAUGHS

Laughter, with us, is no great undertaking;
A sudden wave that breaks and dies in breaking.
Laughter, with Mrs. Reece, is much less simple :
It germinates, it spreads, dimple by dimple,
From small beginnings, things of easy girth,
To formidable redundancies of mirth.

Clusters of subterranean chuckles rise,
And presently the circles of her eyes
Close into slits, and all the woman heaves,
As a great elm with all its mounds of leaves
Wallows before the storm. From hidden sources
A mustering of blind volcanic forces
Takes her and shakes her till she sobs and gapes.
Then all that load of bottled mirth escapes
In one wild crow, a lifting of huge hands
And creaking stays, a visage that expands
In scarlet ridge and furrow. Thence collapse,
A hanging head, a feeble hand that flaps
An apron-end to stir an air and waft
A steaming face. . . . And Mrs. Reece has laughed.

MARTIN ARMSTRONG

PRELUDE TO CRICKET

Before we came the moon-soaked dews were here,
Washing the feet of thrushes while they sang.
No sun was up when this May morning rang
With the first meadow-music of the year.
Those birds had quired their lovely-throated thanks
To see again the world they loved appear,
The cricket ground, the old elm branching clear,
The daisies on the boundary's unscythed banks,
The green pavilion whose hour draws near,
And (lost ball, six !) the green and brackish mere.

God's praise, Spring sweetness ; these, before we came,
Were all : the cool, quiet morning barely stirred.
Now we take on the lease from singing bird,
Assembling here in traffic for a game.
Soon we'll be ready, every man and lad
Tip-toeing, braced how briskly, for the glad
Beginning and the umpire's call of ' Play ! '
Busy beneath the hot, slow-circling sun
We'll carry the morning's echo singing on
With its full gracious flavour in every run
Down to the wicket-drawing close of day.
No frowning combat ours, barren of pranks

And genial moves of venture; lost or won
We'll make it easy, first and last, to find
The clean bright clash of comrades in our match.
All we accomplish, even the bungled catch
Shall challenge joy 'twixt two fresh-flannelled ranks,
Making for summer beauty in the mind
And life's good game when this game's left behind.

And as we crowd its setting to the frame
With lightheart laughter and complete content
We'll think, not birds alone had earlier lease
Of these green acres, rich with grass-lawn scent,
And centred in a groundsman's popping crease.
Even as we pitch our wicket, flickering near
Are shades of men who found this cricket dear
And sealed their happy ventures ere we came.

THOMAS MOULT

FOREFATHERS

Here they went with smock and crook,
  Toiled in the sun, lolled in the shade,
Here they mudded out the brook
  And here their hatchet cleared the glade:
Harvest-supper woke their wit,
Huntsman's moon their wooings lit.

From this church they led their brides,
  From this church themselves were led
Shoulder-high; on these waysides
  Sat to take their beer and bread.
Names are gone—what men they were
These their cottages declare.

Names are vanished, save the few
  In the old brown Bible scrawled;
These were men of pith and thew,
  Whom the city never called;
Scarce could read or hold a quill,
Built the barn, the forge, the mill.

On the green they watched their sons
  Playing till too dark to see,
As their fathers watched them once,
  As my father once watched me;
While the bat and beetle flew
On the warm air webbed with dew.

Unrecorded, unrenowned,
  Men from whom my ways begin,
Here I know you by your ground,
  But I know you not within—
There is silence, there survives
Not a moment of your lives.

Like the bee that now is blown
  Honey-heavy on my hand,
From his toppling tansy-throne
  In the green tempestuous land,—
I'm in clover now, nor know
Who made honey long ago.

EDMUND BLUNDEN

TOWN MAID

As home again I travelled regretfully through London,
She entered. She was pretty, and pranked in all the fashion.
Who can doubt she likes it, her Babylonian bondage, . . .
  The noise, the never-ending streets,
    The pale and clever faces?

Yet as our eyes encountered, I saw her go to milking
Across the unknown meadows until her shoes were golden...
Was it her mother's mother who looked at me, or was it
  No faded ghost, and had I seen,
    Perhaps, her children's children?

CLIFFORD BAX

FRENCH PEASANTS

These going home at dusk
Along the lane,
After the day's warm work,
Do not complain.

Were you to say to them,
'What does it mean?
What is it all about,
This troubled dream?'

They would not understand,
They'd go their way,
Or, if they spoke at all,
They'd surely say,

'Dawn is the time to rise,
Days are to earn
Bread and the mid-day rest,
Dusk to return;

'To be content, to pray.
To hear songs sung,
Or to make wayside love,
If one is young.

'All from the good God comes,
All then is good;
Sorrow is known to Him,
And understood.'

One who had questioned all,
And was not wise,
Might be ashamed to meet
Their quiet eyes.

All is so clear to them,
All is so plain,
These who go home at dusk
Along the lane.

MONK GIBBON

FESTIVAL IN TUSCANY

A low stream by a winding track,
A poplar-bordered plain,
And here at dusk our way was barred
Along a Tuscan lane.

Smoking and jostling peasants lounged
Across the road, and boys
Were larking—yet grew silent when
They heard a silver noise,

And down the lane a bellman came
Ringing a warning bell ;
Then pipes were out and heads were bared,
A grave silence fell.

For here came little maids in white
With veils upon the head,
Small Daughters of the Sacred Heart,
Girded about in red.

So newly born and pure and meek
Singing a psalm or prayer ;
I suddenly saw the first of stars
Dawn in the sallow air.

Then maidens grown and soon to wed,
Tall maidens, two by two,
Daughters of Mary, clad in white,
Girded about with blue.

Black-gowned the wives and mothers walked,
Stark-faced and harrow-lined ;
Under a darkly kerchiefed brow
Their eyes were wise and kind.

Behind them sons and fathers came,
With heavy step they trod ;
Earth-stained and dumb with candles lit,
And after them came God.

Christ on the Cross ! thorns on His brow !
The spear-wound in His side ;
He poured His life into their lives
When He was crucified.

I heard a quaking amid the wheat,
The night began to sigh,
A faint moon shone, a poplar shook
Against an ashen sky ;
The vines leaned out and wrung their hands
When the dead Lord went by.

Lamps on long poles lit up a brow
Blood-stained but aureoled . . .
After that dark and tortured Form,
White-vested, golden-stoled,

The Priest came bearing the sacred Host
Wherein Christ lives again :
We were but heathen, yet we kneeled
While God went down the lane.

WILLIAM FORCE STEAD

THE CICADAS

Sightless, I breathe and touch ; this night of pines
Is needly, resinous and rough with bark.
Through every crevice in the tangible dark
The moonlessness above it all but shines.

Limp hangs the leafy sky ; never a breeze
Stirs, nor a foot in all this sleeping ground ;
And there is silence underneath the trees—
The living silence of continuous sound.

For like inveterate remorse, like shrill
Delirium throbbing in the fevered brain,
An unseen people of cicadas fill
Night with their one harsh note, again, again.

Again, again, with what insensate zest !
What fury of persistence, hour by hour !
Filled with what demon that denies them rest,
Drunk with what source of pleasure and of power !

Life is their madness, life that all night long
Bids them to sing and sing, they know not why ;
Mad cause and senseless burden of their song ;
For life commands and 'life ! ' is all their cry.

I hear them sing, who in the double night
Of clouds and branches fancied that I went
Through my own spirit's dark discouragement,
Deprived of inward as of outward sight ;

Who, seeking, even as here in the wild wood,
A lamp to beckon through my tangled fate,
Found only darkness and, disconsolate,
Mourned the lost purpose and the vanished good.

Now in my empty heart the crickets' shout
Re-echoing denies and still denies
With stubborn folly all my learnêd doubt,
In madness more than I in reason wise.

Life, life! The word is magical. They sing,
And in my darkened soul the great sun shines;
My fancy blossoms with remembered spring,
And all my autumns ripen on the vines.

Life! and each knuckle of the fig tree's pale
Dead skeleton breaks out with emerald fire.
Life! and the tulips blow, the nightingale
Calls back the rose, calls back the old desire.

And old desire that is for ever new,
Desire, life's earliest and latest birth,
Life's instrument to suffer and to do,
Springs with the roses from the teeming earth.

Desire that from the world's bright body strips
Deforming time and makes each kiss the first;
That gives to hearts, to satiated lips
The endless bounty of to-morrow's thirst.

Time passes and the watery moonrise peers
Between the tree-trunks. But no outer light
Tempers the chances of our groping years,
No moon beyond our labyrinthine night.

Clueless we go; but I have heard thy voice,
Divine unreason! harping in the leaves,
And grieve no more; for wisdom never grieves,
And thou hast taught me wisdom; I rejoice.

ALDOUS HUXLEY

FROM 'REQUIEM'

The feathers in a fan
are not so frail as man;
the green embossèd leaf
than man is no more brief.
His life is not so loud
as the passing of a cloud;
his death is quieter
than harebells, when they stir.
The years that have no form
and substance are as warm,
and space has hardly less
supreme an emptiness.
And yet man being frail
does on himself prevail,
and with a single thought
can bring the world to naught,
as being brief he still
bends to his fleeting will
all time, and makes of it
the shadow of his wit.
Soundless in life and death
although he vanisheth,
the echo of a song
makes all the stars a gong.
Cold, void, and yet the grim
darkness is hot with him,
and space is but the span
of the long love of man.

HUMBERT WOLFE

FARE WELL

When I lie where shades of darkness
Shall no more assail mine eyes,
Nor the rain make lamentation
    When the wind sighs;
How will fare the world whose wonder
Was the very proof of me?
Memory fades, must the remembered
    Perishing be?

Oh, when this my dust surrenders
Hand, foot, lip, to dust again,
May these loved and loving faces
    Please other men!
May the rustling harvest hedgerow
Still the Traveller's Joy entwine,
And as happy children gather
    Posies once mine.

Look thy last on all things lovely,
Every hour. Let no night
Seal thy sense in deathly slumber
    Till to delight
Thou have paid thy utmost blessing;
Since that all things thou wouldst praise
Beauty took from those who loved them
    In other days.

WALTER DE LA MARE

MOST LOVELY SHADE

Most lovely Dark, my Æthiopia born
Of the shade's richest splendour, leave not me
Where in the pomp and splendour of the shade
The dark air's leafy plumes no more a lulling music made.

Dark is your fleece, and dark the airs that grew
Amid those weeping leaves.
Plantations of the East drop precious dew
That, ripened by the light, rich leaves perspire.
Such are the drops that from the dark airs' feathers flew.

Most lovely Shade . . . Syrinx and Dryope
And that smooth nymph that changed into a tree
Are dead . . . the shade, that Æthiopia, sees
Their beauty make more bright its treasuries—
Their amber blood in porphyry veins still grows
Deep in the dark secret of the rose
And the smooth stem of many a weeping tree,
And in your beauty grows.

Come then, my pomp and splendour of the shade,
Most lovely cloud that the hot sun made black
As dark-leaved airs,—
Come then, O precious cloud,
Lean to my heart: no shade of a rich tree
Shall pour such splendour as your heart to me.

EDITH SITWELL

THE MOON WORSHIPPERS

We are the partly real ones
Whose bodies are an accident,
Whose half-born souls were never meant
To fix their unsubstantial thrones
Inside a house of blood and bones.

All day we creep about the brain,
Benumbed and deafened with the noise
Of carnal pains and carnal joys,
That thrust their stupid joy and pain
Across the peace of our disdain.

But when the grosser senses swoon,
Then with dances privily,
And the wordless litany,
A million ghosts will importune
Our vestal mistress, lady Moon:

'O undefiled, O lucid Moon,
Hear our attenuated cry!
O little fish of the cold sky,
O swimmer of the void lagoon,
O Moon, shall our release be soon?'

E. R. DODD

THE FOREST-BIRD

The loveliest things of earth are not
Her lilies, waterfalls or trees ;
Or clouds that float like still, white stones
Carved upon azure seas ;
Or snow-white orchids, scarlet-lipped
In darkness of damp woods,
In hush of shadowy leaves ;
Or the pale foam that lights the coast
Of earth on moonless eves.

The moon is lovely, and the sea's
Bright shadow on the sand ;
The phantom vessel as it glides
Out from the phantom land ;
And, hung above the shadowed earth,
Moored in a crystal sky,
That fleet of phantom lights :
These are but beauty's fading flags,
Her perishable delights.

But in transparency of thought
Out of the branched, dark-foliaged word
There flits a strange, soft-glimmering light,
Shy as a forest-bird.
Most lovely and most shy it comes
From realm of sense unknown,
And sings of earthly doom,
Of an immortal happiness
In the soul's deepening gloom.

W. J. TURNER

THE GAY

Those moon-gilded dancers
Prankt like butterflies,
Theirs was such lovely folly
It stayed my rapt eyes :
But my heart that was pondering
Was sadly wise.

To be so lighthearted
What pain was left behind ;
What fetters fallen gave them
Unto this airy mind :
What dark sins were pardoned ;
What God was kind !

I with long anguish bought
Joy that was soon in flight ;
And wondered what these paid
For years of young delight ;
Ere they were born what tears
Through what long night.

All these gay cheeks, light feet,
Were telling over again,
But in a heavenly accent,
A tale of ancient pain
That, the joy spent, must pass
To sorrow again.

I went into the wilderness
Of night to be alone,
Holding sorrow and joy
Hugged to my heart as one,
Lest they fly on those wild ways
And life be undone.

Æ.

DON JUAN'S ADDRESS TO THE SUNSET

Exquisite stillness! What serenities
Of earth and air! How bright atop the wall
The stonecrop's fire, and beyond the precipice
How huge, how hushed the primrose evenfall!
How softly, too, the white crane voyages
Yon honeyed height of warmth and silence, whence
He can look down on islet, lake and shore
And voiceless woods and pathless promontories,
Or, further gazing, view the magnificence
Of cloud-like mountains and of mountainous cloud
Or ghostly wrack below the horizon rim
Not even his eye has vantage to explore.
Now, spirit, find out wings and mount to him,
Wheel where he wheels, where he is soaring soar,
Hang where now he hangs in the planisphere—
Evening's first star and golden as a bee
In the sun's hair—for happiness is here!

ROBERT NICHOLS

TREE PURGE

I, driven, deeper driven in the glade,
As one from blood-guilt (Lord have mercy!)
Flying, seeking sanctuary,
From Fear the Avenger flying to green shade . . .

Your strength, O trees, your stature,
Not by these,
O not by these alone
From the crimson shadow,
From my tormented nature,
Save me, O trees!

I, inward have I known,
Beneath rough bark,
The pulse of the sap, the life-blood in the dark
Pounding, pounding up
From the blind-nurtured root :
Felt those streams course
Through giant trunk and bough with passionless force—
No passion and no fever and no lust—
To where miraculous the green leaves shoot
Skyward, from dust.

I, therefore, to that flood,
I fugitive cry,
Let my tumultuous blood,
Red rivulet in spate
Pricking with lust and turbulent with hate,
A tributary run :
To sink itself and so again be found,
In life not mine washed, overwhelmed and drowned,
All lost,
All won,
Crimson no more, and I no longer I,
In that green channel sucked toward the sun.

GEORGE ROSTREVOR HAMILTON

THEME

The golden eve is all astir,
The tides of sunset flood on us
—Incredible, miraculous—
We look with adoration on
Beauty coming, beauty gone,
That waits not any looking on.

Thoughts will bubble up, and break,
Spilling a sea, a limpid lake,
Into the soul ; and, as they go
—Lightning visitors ! we know
A lattice opened, and the mind
Poised for all that is behind
The lattice, and the poising mind.
Could the memory but hold !
—All the sunsets, flushed with gold,
Are streaming in it !

All the store
Of all that ever was before
Is teeming in it !

All the wit
Of holy living, holy writ,
Waiting till we remember it,
Is dreaming in it !

JAMES STEPHENS

ON MIDDLETON EDGE

If this life-saving rock should fail
Yielding too much to my embrace,
And rock and I to death should race,
The rock would stay there in the dale
While I, breaking my fall,
Would still go on
Further than any wandering star has gone.

ANDREW YOUNG

NORTHERN LIGHT

Here under Heaven ringed
With fingering pale fires
The soul unpacks to lose
Her burden of desires.

Thoughts are the clean gulls,
Flesh cool as a bone,
The mind is a wave here
And the heart a stone.

L. A. G. STRONG

NIGHT PIECE

The Pole, the Bear, and Cassiopeia
So softly shining,
Dark heaven, dark world, to an exquisite dim
Defeat consigning,
Do turn by day away from us, away from us
Their careless faces,
From our golden fire and the triumphs of time
As from time's disgraces.

We are but dew of their dawn, a commodious dew
That life engenders,
Of death and its dark mysterious fears
Getters and spenders,
Whose spirit seeks the wooing air, that wooing air
On heaven reclining
With the Pole, the Bear, and Cassiopeia
Endlessly shining.

A. E. COPPARD

IN TIME LIKE GLASS

In Time like glass the stars are set,
And seeming-fluttering butterflies
Are fixèd fast in Time's glass net
With mountains and with maids' bright eyes.

Above the cold Cordilleras hung
The wingèd eagle and the Moon:
The gold, snow-throated orchid sprung
From gloom where peers the dark baboon:

The Himalayas' white, rapt brows;
The jewel-eyed bear that threads their caves;
The lush plains' lowing herds of cows;
That Shadow entering human graves:

All these like stars in Time are set,
They vanish but can never pass;
The Sun that with them fades is yet
Fast-fixed as they in Time like glass.

W. J. TURNER

THE MIDNIGHT SKATERS

The hop-poles stand in cones,
The icy pond lurks under,
The pole-tops steeple to the thrones
Of stars, sound gulfs of wonder;
But not the tallest there, 'tis said,
Could fathom to this pond's black bed.

Then is not death at watch
Within those secret waters?
What wants he but to catch
Earth's heedless sons and daughters?
With but a crystal parapet
Between, he has his engines set.

Then on, blood shouts, on, on,
Twirl, wheel and whip above him,
Dance on this ball-floor thin and wan,
Use him as though you love him;
Court him, elude him, reel and pass,
And let him hate you through the glass.

EDMUND BLUNDEN

THE SEA

You, you are all unloving, loveless, you;
Restless and lonely, shaken by your own moods,
You are celibate and single, scorning a comrade even,
Threshing your own passions with no woman for the threshing-floor,
Finishing your dreams for your own sake only,
Playing your great game around the world, alone,
Without playmate, or helpmate, having no one to cherish,
No one to comfort, and refusing any comforter.

Not like the earth, the spouse all full of increase
Moiled over with rearing of her many-mouthed young;
You are single, you are fruitless, phosphorescent, cold and callous,
Naked of worship, of love or of adornment,
Scorning the panacea even of labour,
Sworn to a high and splendid purposelessness
Of brooding and delighting in the secret of life's goings,
Sea, only you are free, sophisticated.

You who take the moon in a sieve, and sift
Her flake by flake, and spread her meaning out;
You who roll the stars like jewels in your palm,
So that they seem to utter themselves aloud;
You who steep from out the days their colour,
Reveal the universal tint that dyes
Their web; who shadow the sun's great gestures and expressions
So that he seems a stranger in his passing;
Who voice the dumb night fittingly;
Sea, you shadow of all things, now mock us to death with your shadowing.

D. H. LAWRENCE

LEVIATHAN

I

Leviathan drives the eyed prow of his face,
With the surge dumbly rippling round his lips,
Toward the Atlantid shore ;
Not flat and golden like the Cherubim,
Or a face round and womanish like the Seraphim,
But thick and barbed—the broad, barbed cheeks of Donne.

Beneath he stretched his hands to the sea forests,
Obscure and thick, with the cool freshes under,
Lifts his surprised brows to the sky's milky light,
New come from the abyss.

While a faint radiance, webbed from the waves' substance,
Clung to his changing limbs and his coiled body,
Reddening, making them darker than the sea,
Or half translucent.

And when the mouths of Atlantean brooks
Struck on his mouth with taste of sudden cold
And wound his shoulders like embracing hands,
He put out both thick palms and felt the shallows.

The salt had scurfed his body with white fire
And knotted the rough hair between his breasts,
And as he rose delicate Atlantis trembled,
Tilting upon the sea's plain like a leaf.

The passionless air hung heavy on Atlantis,
And the inclined spears of the flowering bushes
Smoothly dropped down their loosened, threaded petals,
Softening the pathways.

For tideless night had covered her, and sealed
All scent within the narrow throat of flowers,
And sound within the navel of the hills,
And stars in the confusion of the air.

Within her darkness and unconsciousness
She hid all beauty, and her silences
Sound's measures and sequences,
And the black earth quickened
With oppression of blossom.

Ah, thief that swims by night—Leviathan,
Rolled blindly in the wave's trough like a rotting thing,
Come to Atlantis' further edge by dark,
Poised over her quietness ;

Measureless drunkard of the bitter sea,
Insatiate, like some slow stain
Creeping on pleasure's face,
Like sudden misery.

So foul, so desolate,
That you are crept to seek new life,
Have crossed the water's plain,
Desiring and by stealth to gain
For rankness, foolishness and half-conceivèd beauty
Some perfect shape—an Atlantean body.

II

A music met Leviathan returning,
While the still troubled waters of his passage
Dànct every island like a lily head.
Through all the shadowed throats of the wide forest
His unnumbered monster children rode to greet him
On horses winged and dappled over like flowers.

Now huddled waves had lulled their bursting foam
And slight clouds laid their breasts upon the sea ;
The sullen winds, head downward from the sky,
Solicited his movement on their viols.

And the palm trees, heat weary,
Chafing smooth limbs within a rinded shell,
Spoke of his coming with soft acclamation,
Like watchers long grown tired, languid and sorry :

'Look, how he comes'—as faint as whispering deer—
'What storm and state he brings.' Then louder voices,
The unchaste turtles crying out with pleasure,
And badgers from the earth
Sprawled upon the rocks with animal laughter.

'The Cretan bull ferrying across the sea
Bore home no richer load ;
In the reed forest of Eurotas' bank
That quivering swan, clapping strong wings together,
With harsh, sweet voice called out no keener marriage.'
Then shrill response, as seeming from the air,
Invoking joy, summoning desire :

'Hither desires,
Coming as thick and hot as the press and hurry of blood
Striking the apse of the brain,
Ranging abroad, carrying your torches high,
Running as light and remote as a scattered cast of pearls.'

Then antic spirits from the tulip trees :
'We must have tumblers like a wheel of fire.
We must have dancers moving their suave hands :
The tumblers strung backward like a hoop
Until they thrust vermilioned cheeks between their knees.

And the intricacy
Of sweet involving gaiety,
And wine to warm our innocence,
Music to soothe the prickled sense,
Sounding like water or like ringing glass.'

. . . . . .

The mitred Queen of Heaven stirred on her broad, low throne,
Setting the lattice just so much ajar
That wandering airs from earth should cool the room,
Peered down on more-than-Leda and smoothed her wrinkled
snood,
Crying to her Father-Spouse—‘ Dear Lord, how sweet she
looks.’

The clumsy hierarchies,
Wearied by their continual task of praise,
Rested wide heifer eyes upon her fallen lids.
Islanded in stars,
Even the keen Intelligences turned away
From mathematic splendour of the spheres’ incessant, rolling
chime.

Himself, the Father moved,
Traditional and vast,
Remembering fresher years,
Might have inclined his steeply pinnacled head,
But his more zealous Son,
As neat as Thammuz, with smooth, pallid cheeks,
Sensing an evil, shut the casement fast.

· · · · · ·

But I, remembering Atlantis, wept,
Remembering her paths and their unswept flowers,
Clean beaches, patterned by a light sea wrack,
And the ruined halcyon nests that came on shore.

Tears, in their freedom, cloud the eyes,
Drowsing the sense.
Honey and poppy equally mixed together,
They cannot drug away or curtain off with sleep
So many crowding faces,
Such pitiless disharmony of shapes.

PETER QUENNELL

THE MOUNTAIN LAKE

Empty of heart we wait amid the snow,
The feline snow that crouches by the lake.
Empty of heart, except for icy fear
Reflected from unfathomable deeps,
Blue beyond blue, past the inverted pines,
Past mirrored fangs laid bare against the sky,
Past silent air, and silence in the vault,
The iris of the mountain, hiding thought
No human fear might hide, or love reveal
Within the eye, lake of the human soul.

We know this presence. From the valley first
Lifting our eyes toward the mountain wall
We saw the morning tremble in the deep
Where the night's constellations lay dissolved.
We saw the sun, with cautious sword out-thrust,
Creep with that misted blade from height to height,
Testing ravine and bastion and crag
With ringing blows of light. The splintered gold
Broke gaily over forest, lanced the snow
And melted to the valley with delight.

That visible laughter made the earth respond.
An eagle first, immovable above
The highest reach of alp, fluttered its pinions
And then relapsed to stoniness in air.
Larks and cascades competed in their song,
Each conjuring, with throat and rock-foot pool,
A clamour of laughter such as silver makes
Webbed in a girl's gold hair when snaring with it
The first desire of boyhood. From the slopes
Below the alpine panther's drooping pads,
The little cowslips ran like bees disturbed
By a marauding bear. Innumerable flowers
Lifted their heads and flung toward the sun
Their tiny shouts of perfume, breaking together
And deluging the valley with the riot
Of morning-joy indistinguishable from mirth
Of mortal lips and innocence of meadows.

And through this gaiety we took our way
Against the onrush from the slopes above,
Pageant and cavalcade of song and colour,
Dancing and miming of the naked mists
Down through the boulder-rooted woods that stood
Aloof and stubborn, except for the young larches
Who trembled, sighed, and shook their verdant hair.

But all this masquerade from dawn to noon
Borne down against our ascent, could not blind
Our eyes, nor cover the knowledge in our hearts.
We saw, we knew the monster of the ice,
The glacier, the morain of the rocks,
The cleft concealed with a faint feather of snow,
The horror of the silence in the height
Turning to murmur of its own despair.
We knew that as we climbed we should encounter
This powdery spirit like the breath of fear,
Invisible, yet glinting in the air
Above the peak, and shaking through sunshafts
Its venom of resentment on the soul
Of man, of eagle, lark and wild cascade,
The little flowers shouting to the valley,
Frosting them all with leper-touch of terror
Colder than echo, quieter than death.

RICHARD CHURCH

THE SUNFLOWER

See, I have bent thee by thy saffron hair,
    O most strange masker,
Towards my face, thy face so full of eyes,
    O almost legendary monster.
Thee of the saffron, circling hair I bend,
Bend by my fingers knotted in thy hair,
    Hair like broad flames.
So—shall I swear by beech husk, spindle-berry,
To break thee, saffron hair, and peering eye,
    To have the mastery ?

PETER QUENNELL

GLORY

Glory is of the sun, too, and the sun of suns,
and down the shafts of his splendid pinions
run tiny rivers of peace.

Most of his time, the tiger pads and slouches in a burning peace;
And the small hawk high up turns round on the slow pivot of peace.
Peace comes from behind the sun, with the peregrine falcon, and the owl.
Yet all of these drink blood.

D. H. LAWRENCE

SOLSTICES

Worship the summer sun
In the high heavens burning,
While the wheat-filled earth
Ripens, slowly turning
Her swollen sides to his beams,
Until her body teems
With multitudinous birth.

Worship him then, but love
His level winter rays,
That through shy, fireside days
Cool and discreetly move,
With curious, fruitless care
Treading the inner air
Of cavern, house, and den,
Companion to mouse and men.

RICHARD CHURCH

I CLOSED MY EYES TO-DAY AND SAW

I closed my eyes to-day and saw
   A dark land fringed with flame,
A sky of grey with ochre swirls
   Down to the dark land came.

No wind, no sound, no man, no bird,
   No grass, no hill, no wood:
Tall as a pine amid the plain
   One giant sunflower stood.

Its disk was large with ripened seed:
   A red line on the grey,
The flames, as yet afar, I knew
   Would gnaw the world away.

In vain the seeds were ripe; the stem,
   With singed leaves hung around,
Relaxed; and all the big flower stooped
   And stared upon the ground.

WILLIAM FORCE STEAD

MEN FADE LIKE ROCKS

Rock-like the souls of men
   Fade, fade in time.
Falls on worn surfaces
   Slow chime on chime,

Sense, like a murmuring dew,
   Soft sculpturing rain,
Or the wind that blows hollowing
   In every lane.

Smooth as the stones that lie
   Dimmed, water-worn,
Worn of the night and day
   In sense forlorn.

Rock-like the souls of men
   Fade, fade in time;
Smoother than river-rain
   Falls chime on chime.

W. J. TURNER

PSYCHOMETRIST

I listened to a man and he
Had no word to say to me:
Then unto a stone I bowed
And it spoke to me aloud.

'The force that bindeth me so long,
Once sang in the linnet's song;
Now upon the ground I lie,
While the centuries go by!

'Linnets shall for joy atone
And be fastened into stone;
While, upon the waving tree
Stones shall sing in ecstasy!'

JAMES STEPHENS

THE CAGE

Man, afraid to be alive,
Shut his soul in senses five,
From fields of uncreated light
Into the crystal tower of sight,
And from the roaring winds of space
Into the small flesh-carven place
Of the ear whose cave impounds
Only small and broken sounds;
And to this narrow sense of touch
From strength that held the stars in clutch;
And from the warm ambrosial spice
Of flowers and fruits of Paradise
To the frail and fitful power
Of tongue's and nostril's sweet and sour.
And toiling for a sordid wage,
There in his self-created cage
Ah, how safely barred is he
From menace of eternity.

MARTIN ARMSTRONG

THE EXILE

In the dead middle of night,
Quiet and cold,
I heard the screwk of Chantecleer :
Three times he called.
It was an angry signature
Upon the silence scrawled.

Thrice at the frozen hour
He cried his crow,
Waking from dreams of what he was
Millenniums ago,
When, in forests of India,
Under a royal sun,
He with his wives, many and meek,
Lived like Solomon.

Some vestiges remain
Of dreams so deep :
Round his insulted heart
Sick humours creep :
And with his crooked crow he signs
The death-warrant of sleep.

GERALD BULLETT

THE GREATER CATS

The greater cats with golden eyes
Stare out between the bars.
Deserts are there, and different skies,
And night with different stars.
They prowl the aromatic hill,
And mate as fiercely as they kill,
And hold the freedom of their will
To roam, to live, to drink their fill ;
But this beyond their wit know I :
Man lives a little, and for long shall die.

Their kind across the desert range
Where tulips spring from stones,
Not knowing they will suffer change
Or vultures pick their bones.
Their strength's eternal in their sight,
They rule the terror of the night,
They overtake the deer in flight,
And in their arrogance they smite;
But I am sage, if they are strong:
Man's love is transient as his death is long.

Yet oh what powers to deceive!
My wit is turned to faith,
And at this moment I believe
In love, and scout at death.
I came from nowhere, and shall be
Strong, steadfast, swift, eternally:
I am a lion, a stone, a tree,
And as the Polar star in me
Is fixed my constant heart on thee.
Ah, may I stay forever blind
With lions, tigers, leopards, and their kind.

VICTORIA SACKVILLE-WEST

THE SEALS

Leave her alone,
She is the Island's daughter.
Sleek heads, dark heads
Are risen from the water:
Leave her the company
Her songs have brought her.

The old gray music doctors
Of the ocean,
Their holy, happy eyes
Shining devotion,
Applaud and blow
In foam and soft commotion.

It is her hour,
The Island's only daughter.
The dark, sleek heads
Are risen from the water:
Leave her the company
Her songs have brought her.

L. A. G. STRONG

DEATH

Nor dread nor hope attend
A dying animal;
A man awaits his end
Dreaming and hoping all;
Many times he died,
Many times rose again.
A great man in his pride
Confronting murderous men
Casts derision upon
Supersession of breath;
He knows death to the bone—
Man has created death.

W. B. YEATS

THE SIGNATURE OF PAIN

Open the breast :
Heart, physical heart, that mourns in tremours, take it.
Swear to discover the small drop of fire
That makes the body bitter.

Oh, volatile pain !
Regions of earth can offer you no foothold,
Being so gross-compacted. Hosts of heaven,
Invisible spirits from the invisible glory,
Figure the earth to strange intelligence,
Themselves unbodied, bodilessly discerned.
These are the powers of beauty and deep wisdom ;
And pain not least among the hosts of heaven.

Yet if a man should say, ' Here's pain, here's pain !
See by that impress, wind-mark, signature,
By inmost spirit fretting the mind and flesh,
By nature made articulate—see where pain
Reveals the vesture of her divinity.
Follow within. Consider how she broods,
Not perishably born to time and space ;
Pain everlasting, the true self of pain.
Mortals, dismembered into time, conceive
The motion of her presence fragmentary,
With generation, flowering, and decay.
In her own royalty she is pure and constant.
She is the fire that burns within the waters,
Breathes, and by music of its breath creates
Dancing and trembling in the elements.
And, heart, you touch her closest of all creatures :
So by the terror of that altitude
The body melts, grows bitter, and cries peace '—

If a man sees, and worships, and speaks true,
Anatomists hurry busily to confute him ;
Put on clean aprons ; carve a thousand corpses ;
Press out the sap, refine, precipitate ;
Till through the thin and crystal walls there shine
Snowflakes and flowers and diamonds of death.

'In the first flask'—an eloquent old greybeard,
Wagging his nose between a thumb and finger—
'I caught the pain of new-invented airs,
Which if a man should breathe he gripes and throttles
And calls out foolish words. And here are fevers,
Pin-pricks and bullet-wounds and running sores,
Cauteries, amputations. . . . Next to these
Are all the slights that can befall the soul,
As love despised, the marriage-bed betrayed,
Torture of conscience, loss of friends and health'—

Oh, Sir,
This is the *caput mortuum* of pain.
Perhaps your splinters have a power to prickle;
To rend the heart; to open out abysses;
To conjure demons—I believe it true.
They are not pain, for pain is spiritual,
Discerned by spirit, and her signature
Known by the eyes of flesh when spirit has known her.
The inoffensive shining of the sun
Bears witness that he gave her habitation;
For not alone in strength he goes, but peace
Follows his footsteps, and a fostering care.
Even in the shell he comforts the small bird;
Who speaks up manfully and issues forth
To a new world, rejoicing in the sun,
Standing and straddling over the green turf.

If there is understanding, there she walked,
A holy guest. If gentleness and truth,
She gave her blessing. Every countenance
That warms and lights the heart of the beholder
Shews, clear and true, the signature of pain.

ALAN PORTER

THE BOTTLE

Of green and hexagonal glass,
  With sharp, fluted sides—
Vaguely transparent these walls,
  Wherein motionless hides
A simple so potent it can
  To oblivion lull
The weary, the racked, the bereaved,
  The miserable.

Flowers in silent desire
  Their life-breath exhale—
Self-heal, hellebore, aconite
  Chamomile, dwale :
Sharing the same gentle heavens,
  The sun's heat and light,
And, in the dust of their roots,
  The same shallow night.

Each its own livelihood hath,
  Shape, pattern, hue ;
Age on to age unto these
  Keeping steadfastly true ;
And, musing amid them, there moves
  A stranger, named Man,
Who of their ichor distils
  What virtue he can ;

Plucks them ere seed-time to blazon
His house with their radiant dyes ;
Prisons their attar in wax ;
Candies their petals ; denies
Them freedom to breed in their wont ;
Buds, fecundates, grafts them at will ;
And with cunningest leechcraft compels
  Their good to his ill.

Intrigue fantastic as this
  Where shall we find ?
Mute in their beauty they serve him,
  Body and mind.

And one—but a weed in his wheat—
Is the poppy—frail, pallid, whose juice
With its saplike and opiate fume
Strange dreams will induce

Of wonder and horror. And none
Can silence the soul,
Wearied of self and of life,
Earth's darkness and dole,
More secretly, deeply. But finally ?—
Waste not thy breath ;
The words that are scrawled on this phial
Have for synonym, *death*—
Wicket out into the dark
That swings but one way ;
Infinite hush in an ocean of silence
Æons away—
Thou forsaken !—even thou !—
The dread good-bye ;
The abandoned, the thronged, the watched, the unshared—
Awaiting me—I !

WALTER DE LA MARE

GHOSTS

Can they still live,
Beckon and cry
Over the years
After they die
Bringing us grief,
Bringing us tears ?

Those we once set
With us abreast
Shielded and cherished,
Are they distressed
If we forget
After they've perished ?

So while they sleep
Do they not trust
Friendship to keep
Memory bright
Lest it fall quite
Into the dust?

Ah, but they try
That to retain
Lest they should die
Over again.

. . .

What idle cast
Angled his name
Out of dead seas,
So that the past
Stripped of its ease
Filled me with shame?

Out of what space
Echoed his laughter
Back to my ear?
Whence rose his face
Friendly and near
All this time after?

I had been reading.
Rapt, never heeding
How the light crept
Out of the room;
Almost I slept,
Lulled by the gloom.

And did I brood?
No, free from care,
Doubt, or desire—
Such was my mood
Sunk in a chair
Close to the fire.

Almost I slept . . .
Loosely sleep's cords
Over me slipped
Tautened and twined . . .
Then came his words
Back to my mind.

Gently they stole
Wave upon wave
Drawing my soul
Down to his grave:
' You will forget . . .
You will forget . . .'

Then came his eyes
Shining with truth;
Then came his voice
Broken with sighs;
Friend of my choice,
Friend of my youth.

Ah, but I burned
Him to embrace,
Feeling his breath
Hot on my face
So that I yearned
Almost to death;

So that I reeled
Free from sleep's fetters
Out of my chair
Groping to where
I had concealed
Certain old letters.

Holding a candle
Over my head
Thrust I aside
Many a bundle
Labelled and tied
Seeking my dead;

Hearing him yet
Saying ' Goodbye ';
Hearing his sigh
Murmured so low :
' Ah, but I know
You will forget.'

Almost distraught,
Kneeling I sought
Rummaged and fumbled
Straining my eyes :
Then my hand stumbled
On to my prize ;

Buried like him,
Withering under
Many an ashen
Fancy as dim,
Drained of its wonder,
Emptied of passion . . .

So that I wept ;
Strong as a tide
Bitterness swept
Over my head :
I had not cried
When he was dead . . .

. . .

How came this shade
Begging, unbidden
Back to my mind,
Bringing behind
Pain long allayed
Pleasure forgotten ?

Ah, but they live,
Beckon and cry
Over the years
After they die
Bringing us grief,
Bringing us tears.

J. R. ACKERLEY

TO A CHILD IN DEATH

You would have scoffed if we had told you yesterday
  Love made us feel, or so it was with me, like some great bird
    Trying to hold and shelter you in its strong wing;—
A gay little shadowy smile would have tossed us back such a solemn word,
      And it was not for that you were listening
      When so quietly you slipped away
With half the music of the world unheard.
What shall we do with this strange summer, meant for you,—
      Dear, if we see the winter through,
      What shall be done with spring?
This, this is the victory of the Grave; here is death's sting,
That it is not strong enough, our strongest wing.

But what of His who like a Father pitieth?
His Son was also, once, a little thing,
The wistfullest child that ever drew breath,
Chased by a sword from Bethlehem and in the busy house at Nazareth
Playing with little rows of nails, watching the carpenter's hammer swing,
Long years before His hands and feet were tied
And by a hammer and the three great nails He died,
      Of Youth, of Spring,
Of sorrow, of loneliness, of victory the King,
      Under the shadow of that wing.

CHARLOTTE MEW

GIORNO DEI MORTI

Along the avenue of cypresses,
All in their scarlet cloaks and surplices
Of linen, go the chanting choristers,
The priests in gold and black, the villagers . . .

And all along the path to the cemetery
The round dark heads of men crowd silently,

And black-scarved faces of womenfolk, wistfully
Watch at the banner of death, and the mystery.

And at the foot of a grave a father stands
With sunken head, and forgotten, folded hands ;
And at the foot of a grave a mother kneels
With pale shut face, nor either hears nor feels

The coming of the chanting choristers
Between the avenue of cypresses,
The silence of the many villagers,
The candle-flames beside the surplices.

D. H. LAWRENCE

DEATH MAY BE . . .

Death may be very gentle after all :
He turns his face away from arrogant knights
Who fling themselves against him in their fights ;
But to the loveliest he loves to call.
And he has with him those whose ways were mild
And beautiful ; and many a little child.

OLIVER ST. JOHN GOGARTY

THE ATONEMENT

One died upon a lonely Cross
—Lonely enough with two beside.
Dear, that was your loss and my loss,
And it was there we died.
O past the scope of hand's compelling,
Past the cunning of the eyes,
Past the noose that thought, rebelling,
Flings to snare the skies,
His love reached out to every part,
And taught his fellows to atone,
And broke my heart and broke your heart,
And would not let him die alone.

GERALD GOULD

THE HOLLOW MEN

Mistah Kurtz—he dead
A penny for the Old Guy

I

We are the hollow men
We are the stuffed men
Leaning together
Headpiece filled with straw. Alas!
Our dried voices, when
We whisper together
Are quiet and meaningless
As wind in dry grass
Or rats' feet over broken glass
In our dry cellar

Shape without form, shade without colour,
Paralysed force, gesture without motion;

Those who have crossed
With direct eyes, to death's other Kingdom
Remember us—if at all—not as lost
Violent souls, but only
As the hollow men
The stuffed men.

II

Eyes I dare not meet in dreams
In death's dream kingdom
These do not appear:
There, the eyes are
Sunlight on a broken column
There, is a tree swinging
And voices are
In the wind's singing
More distant and more solemn
Than a fading star.

Let me be no nearer
In death's dream kingdom
Let me also wear
Such deliberate disguises
Rat's coat, crowskin, crossed staves
In a field
Behaving as the wind behaves
No nearer—

Not that final meeting
In the twilight kingdom

III

This is the dead land
This is cactus land
Here the stone images
Are raised, here they receive
The supplication of a dead man's hand
Under the twinkle of a fading star.

Is it like this
In death's other kingdom
Waking alone
At the hour when we are
Trembling with tenderness
Lips that would kiss
Form prayers to broken stone.

IV

The eyes are not here
There are no eyes here
In this valley of dying stars
In this hollow valley
This broken jaw of our lost kingdoms

In this last of meeting places
We grope together
And avoid speech
Gathered on this beach of the tumid river

Sightless, unless
The eyes reappear
As the perpetual star
Multifoliate rose
Of death's twilight kingdom
The hope only
Of empty men.

V

Here we go round the prickly pear
Prickly pear prickly pear
Here we go round the prickly pear
At five o'clock in the morning.

Between the idea
And the reality
Between the motion
And the act
Falls the Shadow

For Thine is the Kingdom

Between the conception
And the creation
Between the emotion
And the response
Falls the Shadow

Life is very long

Between the desire
And the spasm
Between the potency
And the existence
Between the essence
And the descent
Falls the Shadow

For Thine is the Kingdom

For thine is
Life is
For Thine is the

This is the way the world ends
This is the way the world ends
This is the way the world ends
Not with a bang but a whimper.

T. S. ELIOT

THE UNFORTUNATE MILLER

On windy days the mill
  Turned with a will,
But on calm days it spread
  Its four sails—dead.

The one-eyed miller man
  Laments that ban,
And to the windless sky
  Turning his vexed eye :

'God help,' he sadly says,
  'This business ;
A hundred days and more
  The wind's forbore,

'And lacking breezes I
  Am bound to die ;
The profit I've forgone
  In offal and grist alone

'Would have bought a cock and a hen,
  A gilt for my pen,
And a row of asters planted
  Just where I wanted ;

'But since the wind is still—
  The devil take the mill !
Never it rains but pours—
  Let's in-a-doors.'

So in-a-doors goes he
  To see—alas to see—
Not the scrapings of pan or pot
  In his famished cot.

The tap of the clock indoors,
  The dusty floors,
His empty crock and purse,
  Made bad seem worse.

He looked at himself in the glass—
  So thin he was!
He looked at the time and date—
  Too late! Too late!

And creeping again to the mill
  That stood stone still,
He tied round his neck the loop
  Of a long dark rope,

Drove a tenpenny nail
  Into the mill's black sail,
Hung his watch on a shelf,
  Then hung himself.

And lo, the wind came! Beshrew,
  How the wind blew!
And the sails, with the miller dying,
  Went flying, flying.

A. E. COPPARD

NOBODY

Nobody, ancient mischief, nobody,
Harasses always with an absent body.

Nobody coming up the road, nobody,
Like a tall man in a dark cloak, nobody.

Nobody about the house, nobody,
Like children creeping up the stairs, nobody.

Nobody anywhere in the garden, nobody,
Like a young girl quiet with needlework, nobody.

Nobody coming, nobody, not yet here,
Incessantly welcomed by the wakeful ear.

Until this nobody shall consent to die,
Under his curse must every man lie—

The curse of his jealousy, of his grief and fright,
Of sudden rape and murder screamed in the night.

ROBERT GRAVES

BELEAGUERED CITIES

Build your houses, build your houses, build your towns,
Fell the woodland, to a gutter turn the brook,
Pave the meadows, pave the meadows, pave the downs,
  Plant your bricks and mortar where the grasses shook,
  The wind-swept grasses shook.
Build, build your Babels black against the sky—
But mark yon small green blade, your stones between,
  The single spy
Of that uncounted host you have outcast;
For with their tiny pennons waving green
  They shall storm your streets at last.

Build your houses, build your houses, build your slums,
  Drive your drains where once the rabbits used to lurk,
Let there be no song there save the wind that hums
  Through the idle wires while dumb men tramp to work,
  Tramp to their idle work.
Silent the siege; none notes it; yet one day
Men from your walls shall watch the woods once more
  Close round their prey.
Build, build the ramparts of your giant-town;
Yet they shall crumble to the dust before
  The battering thistle-down.

F. L. LUCAS

THE RUIN

Gone are the coloured princes, gone echo, gone laughter:
Drips the blank roof: and the moss creeps after.

Dead is the crumbled chimney: all mellowed to rotting
The wall-tints, and the floor-tints, from the spotting
Of the rain, from the wind and slow appetite
Of patient mould: and of the worms that bite
At beauty all their innumerable lives.

—But the sudden nip of knives,
The lady aching for her stiffening lord,
The passionate-fearful bride,
And beaded Pallor clamped to the torment-board,
Leave they no ghosts, no memories by the stairs?
No sheeted glimmer treading floorless ways?
No haunting melody of lovers' airs,
Nor stealthy chill upon the noon of days?

No: for the dead and senseless walls have long forgotten
What passionate hearts beneath the grass lie rotten.

Only from roofs and chimneys pleasantly sliding
Tumbles the rain in the early hours:
Patters its thousand feet on the flowers,
Cools its small grey feet in the grasses.

RICHARD HUGHES

ISHMAEL

'*And God was with the lad; and he grew, and dwelt in the wilderness, and became an archer.'—Genesis xxi* 20.

And Ishmael crouched beside a crackling briar,
Blinded with sand, and maddened by his thirst,
A derelict, though he knew not why accursed.
And lo! One saw, and strung the dissonant lyre,
Made firm his bow unto the arrow's spire,
And gave him dates and wine. Then at the first
Flushings of dawn Ishmael arose, and burst
To triumphing freedom, ran, and eased desire.

His domain was the desert. None tamed him.
None bought nor sold his spirit, though his hand
Dripped red against the dawn and sunset stain.

Thrones melted, kingdoms passed to the world's rim.
But Ishmael scourged the lion in Paran land,
And kept his faith with God. And he will reign.

HERBERT PALMER

SAILING TO BYZANTIUM

That is no country for old men. The young
In one another's arms; birds in the trees,
—Those dying generations—at their song;
The salmon-falls, the mackerel-crowded seas,
Fish, flesh or fowl, commend all summer long
Whatever is begotten, born, and dies.
Caught in that sensual music all neglect
Monuments of unageing intellect.

An aged man is but a paltry thing,
A tattered coat upon a stick, unless
Soul clap its hands and sing, and louder sing
For every tatter in its mortal dress,
Nor is there singing school but studying
Monuments of its own magnificence;
And therefore I have sailed the seas and come
To the holy city of Byzantium.

O sages standing in God's holy fire
As in the gold mosaic of a wall,
Come from the holy fire, perne in a gyre,
And be the singing-masters of my soul.
Consume my heart away; sick with desire
And fastened to a dying animal
It knows not what it is; and gather me
Into the artifice of eternity.

Once out of nature I shall never take
My bodily form from any natural thing,
But such a form as Grecian goldsmiths make
Of hammered gold and gold enamelling
To keep a drowsy emperor awake;
Or set upon a golden bough to sing
To lords and ladies of Byzantium
Of what is past, or passing, or to come.

W. B. YEATS

GERONTION

Thou hast nor youth nor age
But as it were an after dinner sleep
Dreaming of both.

Here I am, an old man, in a dry month,
Being read to by a boy, waiting for rain.
I was neither at the hot gates
Nor fought in the warm rain
Nor knee deep in the salt marsh, heaving a cutlass,
Bitten by flies, fought.
My house is a decayed house,
And the jew squats on the window sill, the owner,
Spawned in some estaminet of Antwerp,
Blistered in Brussels, patched and peeled in London.
The goat coughs at night in the field overhead;
Rocks, moss, stonecrop, iron, merds.
The woman keeps the kitchen, makes tea,
Sneezes at evening, poking the peevish gutter.

I an old man,
A dull head among windy spaces.

Signs are taken for wonders. 'We would see a sign!'
The word within a word, unable to speak a word,
Swaddled with darkness. In the juvescence of the year
Came Christ the tiger

In depraved May, dogwood and chestnut, flowering judas,
To be eaten, to be divided, to be drunk
Among whispers; by Mr. Silvero
With caressing hands, at Limoges
Who walked all night in the next room;
By Hakagawa, bowing among the Titians;
By Madame de Tornquist, in the dark room
Shifting the candles; Fräulein von Kulp
Who turned in the hall, one hand on the door. Vacant shuttles
Weave the wind. I have no ghosts
An old man in a draughty house
Under a windy knob.

After such knowledge, what forgiveness? Think now
History has many cunning passages, contrived corridors
And issues, deceives with whispering ambitions,
Guides us by vanities. Think now
She gives when our attention is distracted
And what she gives, gives with such supple confusions
That the giving famishes the craving. Gives too late
What's not believed in, or if still believed,
In memory only, reconsidered passion. Gives too soon
Into weak hands, what's thought can be dispensed with
Till the refusal propagates a fear. Think
Neither fear nor courage saves us. Unnatural vices
Are fathered by our heroisms. Virtues
Are forced upon us by our impudent crimes.
These tears are shaken from the wrath-bearing tree.

The tiger springs in the new year. Us he devours. Think
at last
We have not reached conclusion, when I
Stiffen in a rented house. Think at last
I have not made this show purposelessly
And it is not by any concitation
Of the backward devils.
I would meet you upon this honestly.
I that was near your heart was removed therefrom
To lose beauty in terror, terror in inquisition.
I have lost my passion: why should I need to keep it
Since what is kept must be adulterated?
I have lost my sight, smell, hearing, taste and touch:
How should I use them for your closer contact?

These with a thousand small deliberations
Protract the profit of their chilled delirium,
Excite the membrane, when the sense has cooled,
With pungent sauces, multiply variety
In a wilderness of mirrors. What will the spider do,
Suspend its operations, will the weevil
Delay? De Bailhache, Fresca, Mrs. Cammel, whirled
Beyond the circuit of the shuddering Bear
In fractured atoms. Gull against the wind, in the windy
straits

Of Belle Isle, or running on the Horn,
White feathers in the snow, the Gulf claims,
And an old man driven by the Trades
To a sleepy corner.
Tenants of the house,
Thoughts of a dry brain in a dry season.

T. S. ELIOT

THE GOLDEN ROOM

Do you remember that still summer evening
When, in the cosy cream-washed living-room
Of The Old Nailshop, we all talked and laughed—
Our neighbours from The Gallows, Catherine
And Lascelles Abercrombie ; Rupert Brooke ;
Eleanor and Robert Frost, living a while
At Little Iddens, who'd brought over with them
Helen and Edward Thomas ? In the lamplight
We talked and laughed ; but, for the most part, listened
While Robert Frost kept on and on and on,
In his slow New England fashion, for our delight,
Holding us with shrewd turns and racy quips,
And the rare twinkle of his grave blue eyes ?

We sat there in the lamplight, while the day
Died from rose-latticed casements, and the plovers
Called over the low meadows, till the owls
Answered them from the elms, we sat and talked :
Now, a quick flash from Abercrombie ; now,
A murmured dry half-heard aside from Thomas ;
Now, a clear laughing word from Brooke ; and then
Again Frost's rich and ripe philosophy,
That had the body and tang of good draught-cider,
And poured as clear a stream.
'Twas in July
Of nineteen-fourteen that we sat and talked ;
Then August brought the war, and scattered us.

Now, on the crest of an Ægean isle,
Brooke sleeps, and dreams of England : Thomas lies
'Neath Vimy Ridge, where he, among his fellows,
Died, just as life had touched his lips to song.

And nigh as ruthlessly has life divided
Us who survive ; for Abercrombie toils
In a black Northern town, beneath the glower
Of hanging smoke ; and in America
Frost farms once more ; and, far from The Old Nailshop,
We sojourn by the Western sea.

And yet,
Was it for nothing that the little room,
All golden in the lamplight, thrilled with golden
Laughter from the hearts of friends that summer night ?
Darkness has fallen on it ; and the shadow
May never more be lifted from the hearts
That went through those black years of war, and live.

And still, whenever men and women gather
For talk and laughter on a summer night,
Shall not that lamp rekindle ; and the room
Glow once again alive with light and laughter ;
And, like a singing star in time's abyss,
Burn golden-hearted through oblivion ?

WILFRID GIBSON

WHEN

When mine hour is come
Let no teardrop fall
And no darkness hover
Round me where I lie.
Let the vastness call
One who was its lover,
Let me breathe the sky.

Where the lordly light
Walks along the world,
And its silent tread
Leaves the grasses bright,
Leaves the flowers uncurled,
Let me to the dead
Breathe a gay good-night.

Æ.

I SIT ALONE

I sit alone,
And clear thoughts move in me,
Pictures, now near, now far,
Of transient fantasy.
Happy I am, at peace
In my own company.

Yet life is a dread thing, too,
Dark with horror and fear.
Beauty's fingers grow cold,
Sad cries I hear,
Death with a stony gaze
Is ever near.

Lost in myself I hide
From the cold unknown:
Lost, like a world cast forth
Into space star-sown:
And the songs of the morning are stilled,
And delight in them flown.

So even the tender and dear
Like phantoms through memory stray—
Creations of sweet desire,
That faith can alone bid stay:
They cast off the cloak of the real
And vanish away.

Only love can redeem
This truth, that delight;
Bring morning to blossom again
Out of plague-ridden night;
Restore to the lost the found,
To the blinded sight.

WALTER DE LA MARE

PROMISE

Be not so desolate
Because thy dreams have flown
And the hall of the heart is empty
And silent as stone,
As age left by children
Sad and alonc.

Those delicate children,
Thy dreams, still endure :
All pure and lovely things
Wend to the Pure.
Sigh not : unto the fold
Their way was sure.

Thy gentlest dreams, thy frailest,
Even those that were
Born and lost in a heart-beat,
Shall meet thee there,
They are become immortal
In shining air.

The unattainable beauty
The thought of which was pain,
That flickered in eyes and on lips
And vanished again :
That fugitive beauty
Thou shalt attain.

The lights innumerable
That led thee on and on,
The Masque of Time ended,
Shall glow into one.
It shall be with thee for ever
Thy travel done.

Æ.

IV

1930–1942

THE STORM CONE

1932

This is the midnight—let no star
Delude us—dawn is very far.
This is the tempest long foretold—
Slow to make head but sure to hold.

Stand by! The lull 'twixt blast and blast
Signals the storm is near, not past;
And worse than present jeopardy
May our forlorn to-morrow be.

If we have cleared the expectant reef,
Let no man look for his relief.
Only the darkness hides the shape
Of further peril to escape.

It is decreed that we abide
The weight of gale against the tide
And those huge waves the outer main
Sends in to set us back again.

They fall and whelm. We strain to hear
The pulses of her labouring gear,
Till the deep throb beneath us proves,
After each shudder and check, she moves!

She moves, with all save purpose lost,
To make her offing from the coast;
But, till she fetches open sea,
Let no man deem that he is free!

RUDYARD KIPLING

AN ACRE OF GRASS

Picture and book remain,
An acre of green grass
For air and exercise,
Now strength of body goes ;
Midnight, an old house
Where nothing stirs but a mouse.

My temptation is quiet.
Here at life's end
Neither loose imagination,
Nor the mill of the mind
Consuming its rag and bone,
Can make the truth known.

Grant me an old man's frenzy,
Myself must I remake
Till I am Timon and Lear
Or that William Blake
Who beat upon the wall
Till Truth obeyed his call ;

A mind Michael Angelo knew
That can pierce the clouds,
Or inspired by frenzy
Shake the dead in their shrouds ;
Forgotten else by mankind,
An old man's eagle mind.

W. B. YEATS

THE OLD MEN

We old men,
We are not what we seem
As we go down the street.

In our old eyes
Shine boyhood memories:
We have seen horses swerve,
And vessels sail,
We know the crimson curve
Upon a young girl's cheek.

When we wake at end of night,
We draw a deeper breath
And hail the Lord of Light.
We are not what we seem,
We are not afraid of death
As we go down the street.

ERNEST RHYS

WHEN I'M ALONE

'*When I'm alone*'—the words tripped off his tongue
As though to be alone were nothing strange.
'*When I was young*,' he said; '*when I was young* . . . '

I thought of age, and loneliness, and change.
I thought how strange we grow when we're alone,
And how unlike the selves that meet, and talk,
And blow the candles out, and say good-night.
Alone . . . The word is life endured and known.
It is the stillness where our spirits walk
And all but inmost faith is overthrown.

SIEGFRIED SASSOON

FULL MOON

As I walked out that sultry night,
I heard the stroke of one.
The moon, attained to her full height,
Stood beaming like the sun:
She exorcised the ghostly wheat
To mute assent in love's defeat,
Whose tryst had now begun.

The fields lay sick beneath my tread,
A tedious owlet cried,
A nightingale above my head
With this or that replied—
Like man and wife who nightly keep
Inconsequent debate in sleep
As they dream side by side.

Your phantom wore the moon's cold mask,
My phantom wore the same;
Forgetful of the feverish task
In hope of which they came,
Each image held the other's eyes
And watched a grey distraction rise
To cloud the eager flame—

To cloud the eager flame of love,
To fog the shining gate;
They held the tyrannous queen above
Sole mover of their fate,
They glared as marble statues glare
Across the tessellated stair
Or down the halls of state.

And now warm earth was Arctic sea,
Each breath came dagger-keen;
Two bergs of glinting ice were we,
The broad moon sailed between;
There swam the mermaids, tailed and finned,
And love went by upon the wind
As though it had not been.

ROBERT GRAVES

A SONG FOR SIMEON

Lord, the Roman hyacinths are blooming in bowls and
The winter sun creeps by the snow hills ;
The stubborn season has made stand.
My life is light, waiting for the death wind,
Like a feather on the back of my hand.
Dust in sunlight and memory in corners
Wait for the wind that chills towards the dead land.

Grant us thy peace.
I have walked many years in this city,
Kept faith and fast, provided for the poor,
Have given and taken honour and ease.
There went never any rejected from my door.
Who shall remember my house, where shall live my children's
    children
When the time of sorrow is come ?
They will take to the goat's path, and the fox's home,
Fleeing from the foreign faces and the foreign swords.

Before the time of cords and scourges and lamentation
Grant us thy peace.
Before the stations of the mountain of desolation,
Before the certain hour of maternal sorrow,
Now at this birth season of decease,
Let the Infant, the still unspeaking and unspoken Word,
Grant Israel's consolation
To one who has eighty years and no to-morrow.

According to thy word.
They shall praise Thee and suffer in every generation
With glory and derision,
Light upon light, mounting the saints' stair.
Not for me the martyrdom, the ecstasy of thought and prayer,
Not for me the ultimate vision.
Grant me thy peace.
(And a sword shall pierce thy heart,
Thine also).
I am tired with my own life and lives of those after me,
I am dying in my own death, and the deaths of those after me.
Let thy servant depart
Having seen thy salvation.

T. S. ELIOT

SISSINGHURST

A tired swimmer in the waves of time
I throw my hands up : let the surface close :
Sink down through centuries to another clime,
And buried find the castle and the rose.
        Buried in time and sleep,
        So drowsy, overgrown,
That here the moss is green upon the stone,
        And lichen stains the keep.
I've sunk into an image, water-drowned,
Where stirs no wind and penetrates no sound,
Illusive, fragile to a touch, remote,
Foundered within the well of years as deep
As in the waters of a stagnant moat.
Yet in and out of these decaying halls
I move, and not a ripple, not a quiver,
Shakes the reflection though the waters shiver,—
My tread is to the same illusion bound.
Here, tall and damask as a summer flower,
Rise the brick gable and the springing tower ;
        Invading Nature crawls
With ivied fingers over rosy walls,
        Searching the crevices,
Clasping the mullion, riveting the crack,
Binding the fabric crumbling to attack,
And questing feelers of the wandering fronds
        Grope for interstices,
Holding this myth together under-seas,
        Anachronistic vagabonds !

And here, by birthright far from present fashion,
As no disturber of the mirrored trance
I move, and to the world above the waters
        Wave my incognisance.

For here, where days and years have lost their number,
I let a plummet down in lieu of date,
And lose myself within a slumber
        Submerged, elate.

For now the apple ripens, now the hop,
And now the clover, now the barley-crop ;
Spokes bound upon a wheel forever turning,
Wherewith I turn, no present manner learning ;
Cry neither ‘ Speed your processes ! ’ nor ‘ Stop ! ’
I am content to leave the world awry
(Busy with politic perplexity,)
If still the cart-horse at the fall of day
Clumps up the lane to stable and to hay,
And tired men go home from the immense
        Labour and life's expense
That force the harsh recalcitrant waste to yield
Corn and not nettles in the harvest-field ;
This husbandry, this castle, and this I
        Moving within the deeps,
Shall be content within our timeless spell,
Assembled fragments of an age gone by,
While still the sower sows, the reaper reaps,
Beneath the snowy mountains of the sky,
And meadows dimple to the village bell.
So plods the stallion up my evening lane
And fills me with a mindless deep repose,
        Wherein I find in chain
The castle, and the pasture, and the rose.

Beauty, and use, and beauty once again
Link up my scattered heart, and shape a scheme
Commensurate with a frustrated dream.

The autumn bonfire smokes across the woods
And reddens in the water of the moat ;
As red within the water burns the scythe,
And the moon dwindled to her gibbous tithe
        Follows the sunken sun afloat.
Green is the eastern sky and red the west ;
The hop-kilns huddle under pallid hoods ;
The waggon stupid stands with upright shaft,
As daily life accepts the night's arrest.
Night like a deeper sea engulfs the land,
The castle, and the meadows, and the farm ;

Only the baying watch-dog looks for harm,
And shakes his chain towards the lunar brand.

In the high room where tall the shadows tilt
As candle flames blow crooked in the draught,
The reddened sunset on the panes was spilt,
But now as black as any nomad's tent
The night-time and night of time have blent
Their darkness, and the waters doubly sleep.
Over my head the years and centuries sweep,
    The years of childhood flown,
    The centuries unknown;
I dream; I do not weep.

VICTORIA SACKVILLE-WEST

A SUNDAY

A child in the Sabbath peace, there—
Down by the full-bosomed river;
Sun on the tide-way, flutter of wind,
Water-cluck,—*Ever . . . for ever . . .*

Time itself seemed to cease there—
The domed, hushed city behind me;
Home how distant! The morrow would come—
But here, no trouble could find me.

A respite, a solacing, deep as the sea,
Was mine. Will it come again? . . . Never? . . .
Shut in the Past is that Sabbath peace, there—
Down by the full-bosomed river.

WALTER DE LA MARE

THE STRAWBERRY PLANT

Above the water, in her rocky niche,
She sat enthroned and perfect ; for her crown
One bud, like pearl, and then two fairy roses
Blanched and yet ardent in their glowing hearts :
One greenish berry spangling into yellow
Where the light touched the seed : one fruit achieved
And ripe, an odorous vermilion ball
Tight with completion, lovingly enclasped
By the close cup whose green chimed with the red,
And showered with drops of gold like Danae :
Three lovely sister leaves as like as peas,
Young but full-fledged, dark, with a little down :
Two leaves that to a matron hue inclined ;
And one the matriarch, that dressed in gold
And flushed with wine, thought her last days her best.
And here and there a diamond of dew
Beamed coolly from the white, smiled from the gold,
Silvered the down, struck lightning from the red.
The overhanging rock forbade the sun,
Yet was she all alight with water-gleams
Reflected, like the footlights at a play :
Perfection's self, and (rightly) out of reach.

RUTH PITTER

EARTHFAST

Architects plant their imagination, weld their poems on rock,
clamp them to the skidding rim of the world and anchor them down to its core;
leave more than the poet's or painter's snail-bright trail on a friable leaf;
can build their chrysalis round them—stand in their sculpture's belly.

They see through stone, they cage and partition air, they crossrig space
with footholds, planks for a dance; yet their maze, their flying trapeze
is pinned to the centre. They write their euclidean music standing
with a hand on a cornice of cloud, themselves set fast, earth-square.

A. S. J. TESSIMOND

GORSE

O fickle as the heart of May,
Was the gorse once so fair?
Who climbed the hill at break of day
To see it flashing there?
Who cut a sprig which far away
Haunted the air?

I cut a sprig, but when the moon
Grew paper-thin and wan,
Its scent declined like an old tune
Half lost, but lingering on;
Or like those words now fresh, but soon
Faded and gone.

HELEN FOLEY

DUCHESS

The trace-horse, watch her move;
She takes the hill as a ship,
Figure-head noble,
Devours the steepening wave.
Forehead of midnight caught
In a brass net she coins the light;
Might sleeked with sweat,
A shoulder firm as marble;
Watch her, the great feet grip
Our ground-swell earth, all's set
For home now, tackle taut;
She leans to the work soberly, with love.

Earth dimmed, she wears the dark;
The last load brushing a star,
Rocks into haven,
Sheds whispering in its wake
Lavender leavings, rich moon catch
Too rare to touch;
Glint hands unhitch
Moth horses silverly graven.
Look at her, gloaming fur
Rope-rough she roams, a witch;
Yonder what cobweb leech
Is milking the pond stealthily black.

The stark days, soon they come;
An old mare under the hedge,
Rump to the blizzard,
Is carved on the year's tomb.
Wind-bitten Duchess, breast
Frost-laced she glows august,
Knows winter's worst,
Lean havoc, storm-shock hazard.
Leave her to rust, nor grudge
This yoke-proud labourer lost;
Scored flank December-fleeced
She conjures the snow softly into bloom.

LILIAN BOWES-LYON

MARCH HARES

I made myself as a tree,
No withered leaf twirling on me;
No, not a bird that stirred my boughs,
As looking out from wizard brows
I watched those lithe and lovely forms
That raised the leaves in storms.

I watched them leap and run,
Their bodies hollowed in the sun
To thin transparency,
That I could clearly see
The shallow colour of their blood
Joyous in love's full flood.

I was content enough
Watching that serious game of love,
That happy hunting in the wood
Where the pursuer was the more pursued,
To stand in breathless hush
With no more life myself than tree or bush.

ANDREW YOUNG

CATS

Cats no less liquid than their shadows
Offer no angles to the wind.
They slip, diminished, neat, through loopholes
Less than themselves; will not be pinned

To rules or routes for journeys; counter
Attack with non-resistance; twist
Enticing through the curving fingers
And leave an angered, empty fist.

They wait obsequious as darkness
Quick to retire, quick to return;
Admit no aim or ethics; flatter
With reservations; will not learn

To answer to their names; are seldom
Truly owned till shot or skinned.
Cats, no less liquid than their shadows
Offer no angles to the wind.

A. S. J. TESSIMOND

THE MOTHS

The narrow paths beside the flower-beds run,
Filled full with flowers by the autumn sun,
And the flint wall still casts a shadowy light
Although the blue September day is done.

Among the flowers, soft blurs of misty white
Poised steady on their slow vibrating flight,
Late summer's moths, that face the shortening days,
Dance through the chilled mists of the autumn night.

The darkness deepens still. Clouds hide the sky,
And on the pond the moorhens splash and cry
With their wild voices of an unknown world.
Crunching the flints, a shepherd passes by.

The smoking lantern throws its moving rays
Across the orchard, and the warm light plays
On all the silver undersides of leaves
Of pear and apple trees beside the ways.

The lantern closes, leaves an instant's dark,
Then lights the brown beads on the pear tree's bark
And the drugged moths, with softly quivering wings
Or drowsy, like some lechered knot or mark.

The night, from depths of wood and fields, may bring
Strange, unknown, painted moths, and anything
May be revealed within that splash of light,
Pale wainscot, crimson of red underwing.

And so, from tree to tree, the garden round,
The night dead quiet, and the only sound
A hunting owl across the rush-grown field,
The thud of apples falling to the ground.

JULIAN BELL

THE LOOKER-ON

. . . And ladders leaning against damson trees,
And idle spades beside old garden walls,
And broken sickles covered up in leaves,
And baskets wet with dew, waist deep in grass,
And spider webs across half-open gates . . .
  And memory of a moon, a giant rolling,
And, brown in moon's noonday, prolific oaks,
Glint of moonsilver on their solid acorns . . .
  And a fierce sun melting the fringed horizon,
Cold grass, hard apples fallen and forgotten,
And dew-logged thistledown . . . And crackling beechmast,
And plump matt mushrooms—beggars' harvest—white
As chalk, bland as a nut, and pink to break . . .
  And bonfire incense, and bracken gold as beech,
And bearded hedges, latest blackberries,
Half-ploughed stubble and dusty threshing yards,
And early nights, cloud multitudes on fire . . .
Dry noons, drenched dawns, deep scents, bright stars, lost thoughts . . .
  And empty orchards and wide open fields,
And robin solos in deserted woods,
And chimney smoke, and starry candlelight,
And far-off fields, and distance like the past,
And mossy silence, and the scent of leisure,
And spider webs across half-open gates,
And broken sickles buried under leaves,
And idle spades beside old garden walls,
And ladders leaning against damson trees, . . .

FRANK KENDON

AUTUMN

I love to see, when leaves depart,
The clear anatomy arrive,
Winter, the paragon of art,
That kills all forms of life and feeling
Save what is pure and will survive.

Already now the clanging chains
Of geese are harnessed to the moon:
Stripped are the great sun-clouding planes:
And the dark pines, their own revealing,
Let in the needles of the noon.

Strained by the gale the olives whiten
Like hoary wrestlers beat with toil
And, with the vines, their branches lighten
To brim our vats where summer lingers
In the red froth and sun-gold oil.

Soon on our hearth's reviving pyre
Their rotted stems will crumble up:
And like a ruby, panting fire,
The grape will redden on your fingers
Through the lit crystal of the cup.

ROY CAMPBELL

THE DISCOVERY

Once I found riches here,
  Hidden and snugged with shadowy craft:
So startling quiet, my very stare
  Seemed a delectable theft.

Now with the rags of leaf
  There moulders in the rain and sun,
Thrown slant and thorn-impaled, a sheaf
  Of twigs and floats of down:

The ruins of a nest,
  Last spring a home from the weather, rich
With love when that small wayside breast
  Brooded its heavenly clutch.

STANLEY SNAITH

THE STOCKDOVES

They rose up in a twinkling cloud
And wheeled about and bowed
To settle on the trees
Perching like small clay images.

Then with a noise of sudden rain
They clattered off again
And over Ballard Down
They circled like a flying town.

Though one could sooner blast a rock
Than scatter that dense flock
That through the winter weather
Some iron rule has held together,

Yet in another month from now
Love like a spark will blow
Those birds the country over
To drop in trees, lover by lover.

ANDREW YOUNG

THE SWANS

Only to those who have climbed the dusky hill
To watch the simple contortions of the land
At evening, a beautiful and calm apparel
For our thought, and the mature light
Fallen slanting among trees, shaping them
Palpably, the thought itself the richness
And the consistence of sensitive life;

Only then at last in the moment ordained
By cast of beauty, the swans come: silverly skeined
Above the water's deepened animation,
Their hard unplaceable distant susurrus of wings
Mixing most gently with the sun-sifted birches'
Light behaviour and the childish wind's agility.

Only then caught in the shock of wonder,
Folding again with easy rings, the surface
Of contention shows an equal image
Stealing white in the enclosing river's incredible silk
At the grey conclusion of flight,
The locked wings, the calmed heart.

RANDALL SWINGLER

GULLS

How gentle and how friendly seem
  The bright guests of the plough,
Following the furrow up and down
  And parleying as they go.

Yet of all creatures most aloof
  Are these cliff-nurseried things,
Patrolling inland with the threat
  Of tempest in their wings.

STANLEY SNAITH

BURNING THE BEE-TREE

Lay on the fire their ancient hold,
Which they left when the tree died :
We threw their tower down on the mould,
And split it open wide,
But they had taken away their gold,
And there was none inside.

Nothing but the embalming stain,
And a few shards of comb,
And a breath as of the clover-plain
Still lingered in their home,
With skeletons of robbers slain,
Who had too rich a tomb.

Up sweetly on the autumn air
Spiced funeral vapours rise :
What do you see above, what fair
Visions salute your eyes,
What reverend memories repair
The breach of centuries ?

I smell the death of song, I hear
That fair bird's last lament ;
I see the shades of heroes near,
About their purple tent ;
I see the rich, the dabbled hair,
The damasked armour rent.

And pure, on humble air, the song
Of love is heard to chime,
The oak's unchanging leaves among
In an unchanging rhyme,
For the bees remain the same so long
They keep no count of time.

The labour, and the bitter sting,
The cell's meticulous range,
Honey, which makes a perishing thing
Immortal, do not change ;
Life, make one couplet that I sing
As deathless, and as strange !

RUTH PITTER

THE SCYTHE

This morning as the scythe swung in my grasp
I thought of the sinewy craft my fathers plied,
Those men whose hedgerow name has come to me,
Those soil-bred Yorkshiremen who fashioned snathes.
They lopped and barked and seasoned the leafy staff
To bear the blade with balance. There is a stern
Puritan cleanness in a true-made scythe.
A scythe purges the hands of awkwardness.
It has its own instinct, a subtle weighting
That pulls it round in a rich curve of motion;
And when the steel, fined to a creepy edge,
Rips and rings through the stalks, and the swathe sighs over,
And the cropped circle widens at each stroke,
What a singing power flows from the hands!
The old rhythm came smoothly to my wrist.
I seemed to feel my ancestry move within me.
For though I left their soil, I found a craft
Nourished with a tradition choice as theirs:
They toiled in wood, I curb the grain of words,
Both winning grace and service from what's wild.
Scythe and sentence share one craftsmanship.

STANLEY SNAITH

TO MY BLACKTHORN STICK

When sap ebbed low and your green days were over—
Hedging a gap to rugged land,
Bare skinned and straight you were; and there I broke you
To champion my right hand.

Well shod in bronze and lithe with hillside breeding,
Yet, like a snarl, you dogged my side,
Mailed in your tridents and flaunting out the fierceness
That bristled through your hide.

So armed as one, have we not shared each journey
On noiseless path or road of stone;
O exiled brother of the flowering sloe tree,
Your past ways are my own.

Lonesome, like me, and song-bred on Mount Nephin,
You, also, found that in your might
You broke in bloom before the time of leafing
And shocked a world with light.

But you grew shy,—eyed through by glowering twilights—
Sharing the still of night's grey brew,
Secret and shy, while things unseen were sighing
Their grass tunes under you.

Manured with earth's own sweat you stretched in saplings;
Seasoned, you cored your fruit with stone;
Then stript in fight, your strength came out of wrestling
All winds by winter blown.

I took that strength; my axe blow was your trumpet,
You rose from earth, god-cleaned and strong;
And here, as in green days you were the perch,
You're now the prop of song.

F. R. HIGGINS

THE FALCON AND THE DOVE

This high-caught hooded Reason broods upon my wrist,
Fettered by a so tenuous leash of steel.
We are bound for the myrtle marshes, many leagues away,
And have a fair expectation of quarry.

Over the laggard dove, inclining to green boscage
Hovers this intentional doom—till the unsullied sky receives
A precipitation of shed feathers
And the swifter fall of wounded wings.

Will the plain aye echo with that loud *bullallo*
Or retain an impress of our passage?
We have caught Beauty in a wild foray
And now the falcon is hooded and comforted away.

HERBERT READ

DUST

The sower trudged and swung, leaning
 On the sinewy wind, and as he tossed,
The grain over the chapped furrows
 Puffed from his hand like dust.

Dragged and riven, the upland trees
 Went in confusion of leaf;
Even the pedantic oaks
 Bowed to that shadowy mischief.

Last autumn's skeletons ran, or lifted
 Like a flirt of sparrows off the ground.
I dizzied at that tangled flight
 And the woodland's surf-sound.

O Conqueror, stand awhile in the hills
 Before scattering my life, I said,
With the dead leaves and the quick dust
 And the thoughts out of my head.

STANLEY SNAITH

A CHILD ASLEEP

Angel of Words, in vain I have striven with thee,
Nor plead a lifetime's love and loyalty;
Only, with envy, bid thee watch this face,
 That says so much, so flawlessly,
 And in how small a space!

WALTER DE LA MARE

MIDNIGHT

I have thrown wide my window
And looked upon the night,
And seen Arcturus burning
In chaos, proudly bright.

The powdered stars above me
Have littered heaven's floor—
A thousand I remember;
I saw a myriad more.

I have forgotten thousands
For deep and deep between,
My mind built up the darkness
Of space, unheard, unseen.

I held my hands to heaven
To hold perfection there,
But through my fingers streaming
Went time, as thin as air;

And I must close my window
And draw a decent blind
To screen from outer darkness
The chaos of the mind.

MICHAEL ROBERTS

CLIO

Something so noble in that lifted brow,
Exchanging arrows with the morning light—
Even as one caught the gleam, it seemed that now
The day was come, imperial, out of night.
For she could break the dark, and lend to age
Outrageous youth and lover's ecstasy.
Spring's taunting woodlands were her heritage,
Song in her voice, that rang the reverie.
Indeed I thought the Golden Bough was hers,
That dropt its petals at the gate of death ;
And being woman, she had woman's tears
To break the heart, or heal it at a breath.
Last, in her secret self, she kept the seal
And soul of things—the unattainable.

ERNEST RHYS

I THINK MYSELF TO BE ALIVE

I think myself to be alive,
Yet died I not that summer night
When in her arms I lay ?
And knew indeed that joy should kill,
And stayed so till the day,
And prayed so till the day.

I think myself to be alive,
Now in the dying winter light
When winter-time has come,
Now pain has writhen heart and limb,
And the little tits are dumb,
The little souls are dumb.

DOROTHY WELLESLEY

CHILDLESS

Call to the swan and bid him bring
A blessing from his plumy thigh
For one that tires of whispering
    To heaven, as I.

Let that fierce eye and urgent breast
Disparage all my tumbled shape
Beneath the imperious webs opprest:
    From throat to nape

Slide the long neck and hissing head,
Torment my bosom in his bill,
Awaking all that now is dead
    To do his will.

L. A. G. STRONG

THE BRIDE

The fight that was no fight is over,
The uncontested victory won;
The conqueror, sleeping by her side,
Forgets already what is done.

But she, a pulse of deeper being,
Death's wakeful foe from age to age,
In the great army of creation
Enrols and takes her heritage.

L. A. G. STRONG

A SON IN DECEMBER

Last March, an angel of the night,
Love entered with the man I love,
Woke me from sleep for his delight,
And strongly with my virtue strove;

And I, feeling his strength of God,
Let him dissolve me with his fire,
And never suffered dearer load
Than pillowing his forspent desire.

Now, here, in homely-scented straw,
December brings me my release:
Racked by every breath I draw,
A great pain, a greater peace.

What if I cry? A fainter cry
Shall more than heal this rending soon,
And two shall sleep, my son and I,
Here in the straw where lies but one.

In each black outer night of fear
This living love, this core of proof,
Binds to my thought a single star,
Bright and remote above the roof;

It sets the seal of womankind—
A paradox of joy and pain,
The diamond of a yielding mind—
On blood of mine, my heart, my brain.

O body, whose timidity
Love honoured then, be iron now;
Burst through this dark that threatens me;
O Life, be born, I know not how!

There comes an end to pain at last;
I breathe, I watch my thoughts like dreams;
Sleep in my nerves, and in the vast
Room of the world about my limbs.

Let but this choir to silence fade.
Now, while I hear the stars go by,
Bring me the son that I have made;
For he must sleep as well as I. . . .

Love dreamed, I see, of hands, and feet—
Small to perfection.
Do not take him;
This is the last sleep we shall get!
He is himself. The world will wake him.

FRANK KENDON

CRADLE SONG

Out in the dark something complains,
Is it the wild dove's purr?
And there a thing creeps, is it the rain
Eavesdropping near our door?
Then sleep, sleep, my darling—
Sleep until the bow-legged crows
Walk the fields of barley.

May nothing nose the gentle birds,
Abroad in the crawl of night,
Nor the cock, with wings upon his spurs,
Until the peep of light;
Then sleep to my long rocking;
Sleep as the little winds that sleep
All safely in God's pocket—
Yes, safely in God's pocket,
Sleep, my darling.

F. R. HIGGINS

THE ZULU GIRL

When in the sun the hot red acres smoulder,
Down where the sweating gang its labour plies,
A girl flings down her hoe, and from her shoulder
Unslings her child tormented by the flies.

She takes him to a ring of shadow pooled
By thorn-trees : purpled with the blood of ticks,
While her sharp nails, in slow caresses ruled,
Prowl through his hair with sharp electric clicks,

His sleepy mouth, plugged by the heavy nipple,
Tugs like a puppy, grunting as he feeds ;
Through his frail nerves her own deep languors ripple
Like a broad river sighing through its reeds.

Yet in that drowsy stream his flesh imbibes
An old unquenched unsmotherable heat—
The curbed ferocity of beaten tribes,
The sullen dignity of their defeat.

Her body looms above him like a hill
Within whose shade a village lies at rest,
Or the first cloud so terrible and still
That bears the coming harvest in its breast.

ROY CAMPBELL

THE SCORPION

Limpopo and Tugela churned
In flood for brown and angry miles
Melons, maize, domestic thatch,
The trunks of trees and crocodiles ;

The swollen estuaries were thick
With flotsam, in the sun one saw
The corpse of a young negress bruised
By rocks, and rolling on the shore,

Pushed by the waves of morning, rolled,
Impersonally among shells,
With lolling breasts and bleeding eyes,
And round her neck were beads and bells.

That was the Africa we knew,
Where, wandering alone,
We saw, heraldic in the heat,
A scorpion on a stone.

WILLIAM PLOMER

HORSES ON THE CAMARGUE

In the grey wastes of dread,
The haunt of chattered gulls where nothing moves
But in a shroud of silence like the dead,
I heard a sudden harmony of hooves,
And, turning, saw afar
A hundred snowy horses unconfined,
The silver runaways of Neptune's car
Racing, spray-curled, like waves before the wind.
Sons of the Mistral, fleet
As him with whose strong gusts they love to flee,
Who shod the flying thunders on their feet
And plumed them with the snortings of the sea;
Theirs is no earthly breed
Who only haunt the verges of the earth
And only on the sea's salt herbage feed—
Surely the great white breakers gave them birth.
For when for years a slave,
A horse of the Camargue, in alien lands,
Should catch some far-off fragrance of the wave
Carried far inland from his native sands,
Many have told the tale
Of how in fury, foaming at the rein,
He hurls his rider; and with lifted tail,
With coal-red eyes and cataracting mane,
Heading his course for home,
Though sixty foreign leagues before him sweep,
Will never rest until he breathes the foam
And hears the native thunder of the deep.

But when the great gusts rise
And lash their anger on these arid coasts,
When the scared gulls career with mournful cries
And whirl across the waste like driven ghosts:
When hail and fire converge,
The only souls to which they strike no pain
Are the white-crested fillies of the surge
And the white horses of the windy plain.
Then in their strength and pride
The stallions of the wilderness rejoice;
They feel their Master's trident in their side,
And high and shrill they answer to his voice.
With white tails smoking free,
Long streaming manes, and arching necks, they show
Their kinship to their sisters of the sea—
And forward hurl their thunderbolts of snow.
Still out of hardship bred,
Spirits of power and beauty and delight
Have ever on such frugal pastures fed
And loved to course with tempests through the night.

ROY CAMPBELL

THE SPELL OF FRANCE

Little enough of that wide country,
    Though fascinated long,
Have I as yet acquired: that little
    Is constant undersong,
Astonishment, rest, recognition,
    In my life's round;
And whether I will or no my silence
    Reverts to that bright ground.

First, was it? from the verse of poets
    Who, intimate and shy,
Unveiled the squares, the fairs, the lovers
    Under that calm blue sky,
I thought I won some understanding
    Of the different lure
And look and consonance of life there,
    —And those first dreams endure.

Thereafter, currented with million others
  To history's roaring weirs,
I still found moments, and lacked not feelings,
  Some hours of smiles or tears,
To taste the elixir of that country,
  To kiss the garment's hem,
And, hurled away no matter how fiercely,
  To hoard more than one gem.

Thus now it comes, and from blest occasion
  Of later date though brief,
That some deep music from that country
  Shakes me like a leaf,
And the happy storm of dreams or pictures
  Origined there
Will occupy my whole existence
  And seem my native air.

What else would you, could I? Endeavour
  To number and right-dress
The outward tokens of this passion
  Would be but foolishness:
To name (though sweet the names) each city
  And village of that dream,
Each woodride, each château, each rampart,
  Quarry and cliff and stream;

To summon up lost children's laughter,
  And farmers' terse good talks,
Cassock and sermon in gaunt cool churches,
  Golden past-harvest walks,
Dry veterans garrulous at small tables,
  Bugles and horns and bells—
How might I by these hints create you
  Lord of my spell of spells?

EDMUND BLUNDEN

THOSE IMAGES

What if I bade you leave
The cavern of the mind ?
There's better exercise
In the sunlight and wind.

I never bade you go
To Moscow or to Rome.
Renounce that drudgery,
Call the Muses home.

Seek those images
That constitute the wild,
The lion and the virgin,
The harlot and the child.

Find in middle air
An eagle on the wing,
Recognise the five
That make the Muses sing.

W. B. YEATS

SKY-WIDE AN ESTUARY

Sky-wide an estuary of light
Ebbs amid cloud banks out of sight.
At her star-anchorage shall swing
Earth, the old freighter, till morning.

Ride above your shadow and trim
Cargo till stars grow dim :
Weigh then from the windless river ;
You've a treasure to deliver.

Behold the incalculable seas
Change face for every cloud and breeze :
But a prime mover works inside,
The constant the integral tide.

Though black-bordered fancies vex
You and veering moods perplex,
Underneath's a current knowing
Well enough what way it's going.

Stroked by their windy shadows lie
The grainlands waving at the sky.
That golden grace must all be shed
To fill granaries, to make bread.

Do not grieve for beauty gone.
Limbs that ran to meet the sun
Lend their lightness to another;
Child shall recreate the mother.

CECIL DAY LEWIS

THOUGH BODIES ARE APART

Though bodies are apart,
The dark hours so confine
And fuse our hearts, sure, death
Will find no way between.

Narrow this hour, that bed;
But room for us to explore
Pain's long-drawn equator,
The farthest ice of fear.

Storm passes east, recurs:
The beakéd lightnings stoop:
The sky falls down: the clouds
Are wrung to the last drop.

Another day is born now.
Woman, your work is done.
This is the end of labour.
Come out into the sun!

CECIL DAY LEWIS

REST FROM LOVING

Rest from loving and be living,
Fallen is fallen past retrieving
The unique flyer dawn's dove
Arrowing down feathered with fire.

Cease denying, begin knowing.
Comes peace this way here comes renewing
With dower of bird and bud knocks
Loud on winter wall on death's door.

Here's no meaning but of morning.
Naught soon of night but stars remaining,
Sink lower, fade, as dark womb
Recedes creation will step clear.

CECIL DAY LEWIS

LAY YOUR SLEEPING HEAD

Lay your sleeping head, my love,
Human on my faithless arm ;
Time and fevers burn away
Individual beauty from
Thoughtful children, and the grave
Proves the child ephemeral :
But in my arms till break of day
Let the living creature lie,
Mortal, guilty, but to me
The entirely beautiful.

Soul and body have no bounds :
To lovers as they lie upon
Her tolerant enchanted slope
In their ordinary swoon,
Grave the vision Venus sends
Of supernatural sympathy,
Universal love and hope ;
While an abstract insight wakes
Among the glaciers and the rocks
The hermit's sensual ecstasy.

Certainty, fidelity
On the stroke of midnight pass
Like vibrations of a bell,
And fashionable madmen raise
Their pedantic boring cry ;
Every farthing of the cost,
All the dreaded cards foretell
Shall be paid, but from this night
Not a whisper, not a thought,
Not a kiss nor look be lost.

Beauty, midnight, vision dies :
Let the winds of dawn that blow
Softly round your dreaming head
Such a day of sweetness show
Eye and knocking heart may bless,
Find the mortal world enough ;
Noons of dryness see you fed
By the involuntary powers,
Nights of insult let you pass
Watched by every human love.

W. H. AUDEN

LEAVING BARRA

The dazzle on the sea, my darling,
Leads from the western channel
A carpet of brilliance taking
My leave for ever of the island.

I never shall visit that island
Again with its easy tempo—
The seal sunbathing, the circuit
Of gulls on the wing for garbage.

I go to a different garbage
And scuffle for scraps of notice,
Pretend to ignore the stigma
That stains my life and my leisure.

For fretful even in leisure
I fidget for different values,
Restless as a gull and haunted
By a hankering after Atlantis.

I do not know that Atlantis
Unseen and uncomprehended,
Dimly divined but keenly
Felt with a phantom hunger.

If only I could crush the hunger,
If only I could lay the phantom,
Then I should no doubt be happy
Like a fool or a dog or a buddha.

O the self-abnegation of Buddha,
The belief that is disbelieving,
The denial of chiaroscuro
Not giving a damn for existence!

But I would cherish existence,
Loving the beast and the bubble,
Loving the rain and the rainbow,
Considering philosophy alien.

For all the religions are alien
That allege that life is a fiction,
And when we agree in denial
The cock crows in the morning.

If only I could wake in the morning
And find I had learned the solution,
Wake with the knack of knowledge
Who as yet have only an inkling.

Though some facts foster the inkling—
The beauty of the moon and music,
The routine courage of the worker,
The gay endurance of women,

And you who to me among women
Stand for so much that I wish for,
I thank you, my dear, for the example
Of living like a fugue and moving.

For few are able to keep moving,
They drag and flag in the traffic;
While you are alive beyond question,
Like the dazzle on the sea, my darling.

LOUIS MACNEICE

THE PHŒNIX ANSWERED

Sitting in this garden you cannot escape symbols,
Take them how you will.
Here on the lawn like an island where the wind is still,
Circled by tides in the field and swirling trees,
It is of love I muse,
Who designs the coloured fronds and heavy umbels,
Second-hand marriage, not for passion but business,
Brought on by the obliging bees.

This hedge is a cool perch for the brown turtle-dove,
His phœnix unseen:
Such was their love that perhaps they grew to be one.
At first the mystical making one in marriage
Had all my heart and my homage:
A fire and a fusion were what I wanted of love.
But bodies are separate, and her fanatic bliss
Left the phœnix bodiless.

Frosty burning cloud, delectable gate
Of heaven hopelessly far,
Though tilting almost to touch, whose holy fire
Has no corrosive property unless
Despair of it destroys us;
When we love, toward you our faces are set.
Once I would win by the pains of passion alone,
Aim at you still, that method outgrown.

If daily love now takes from these earlier ones
The sweetness without the pain,
The burning nights, the breathless fears gone,
Peace in their place I never hoped to be given
Unless if ever in heaven—
This is your own success, who have at once
The unscathing fire and the ease of peace,
All that I praise and bless.

ANNE RIDLER

MEETING POINT

Time was away and somewhere else,
There were two glasses and two chairs
And two people with the one pulse
(Somebody stopped the moving stairs):
Time was away and somewhere else.

And they were neither up nor down,
The stream's music did not stop
Flowing through heather, limpid brown,
Although they sat in a coffee shop
And they were neither up nor down.

The bell was silent in the air
Holding its inverted poise—
Between the clang and clang a flower,
A brazen calyx of no noise:
The bell was silent in the air.

The camels crossed the miles of sand
That stretched around the cups and plates;
The desert was their own, they planned
To portion out the stars and dates:
The camels crossed the miles of sand.

Time was away and somewhere else.
The waiter did not come, the clock
Forgot them and the radio waltz
Came out like water from a rock:
Time was away and somewhere else.

Her fingers flicked away the ash
That bloomed again in tropic trees:
Not caring if the markets crash
When they had forests such as these,
Her fingers flicked away the ash.

God or whatever means the Good
Be praised that time can stop like this,
That what the heart has understood
Can verify in the body's peace
God or whatever means the Good.

Time was away and she was here
And life no longer what it was,
The bell was silent in the air
And all the room a glow because
Time was away and she was here.

LOUIS MACNEICE

POLITICS

'*In our time the destiny of man presents its meaning in political terms.*'—THOMAS MANN.

How can I, that girl standing there,
My attention fix
On Roman or on Russian
Or on Spanish politics ?
Yet here's a travelled man that knows
What he talks about,
And there's a politician
That has read and thought,
And maybe what they say is true
Of war and war's alarms,
But O that I were young again
And held her in my arms !

W. B. YEATS

NOW YOU ARE IN YOUR COUNTRY

Now you are in your country,
  And I, locked fast in mine,
Walk the white road in silence,
  And see my sun decline.

I see the whole west breaking
  In flame again, to-night;
And earth to peace receding
  Through valleys of delight.

Sleep, in your pleasant country,
  Lie down at last, content,
The hills of constant heaven
  Your dream's bright battlement;

Know that the stars you talk with
  Have eyes on fields at home,
Or buds on banks you dream of
  Now break in scented foam;

For death has hung no silence
  Nor spring withheld one sign,
Since you turned to your country
  And left me locked in mine.

FRANK KENDON

DAYBREAK

At dawn she lay with her profile at that angle
Which, sleeping, seems the stone face of an angel;
Her hair a harp the hand of a breeze follows
To play, against the white cloud of the pillows.
Then in a flush of rose she woke, and her eyes were open,
Swimming with blue through the rose flesh of dawn.
From her dew of lips, the drop of one word
Fell, from a dawn of fountains, when she murmured
'Darling,'—upon my heart the song of the first bird.
'My dream glides in my dream,' she said, 'come true.
I waken from you to my dream of you.'
O, then my waking dream dared to assume
The audacity of her sleep. Our dreams
Flowed into each other's arms, like streams.

STEPHEN SPENDER

THE VASE OF TEARS

Tears pouring from this face of stone,
Angels from the heart, unhappiness
From some dream to yourself unknown—
Let me dry your eyes with these kisses.
I pour what comfort of ordinariness
I can; faint light upon your night alone.
And then we smother with caresses
Both our starved needs to atone.

Stone face creased with human tears: yet
Something in me gentle and delicate
Sees through those eyes an ocean of green water
And one by one the bitter drops collects
Into my heart, a glass vase which reflects
The world's grief weeping in its daughter.

STEPHEN SPENDER

CURTAIN

Goodbye.
            Incredulously the laced fingers loosen,
Slowly, sensation by sensation, from their warm interchange,
And stiffen like frosted flowers in the November garden.
Already division piles emphasis like bullets ;
Already the one dark air is separate and strange.

Goodbye.
            There is no touch now.   The wave has broken
That for a moment charged the desolate sea.
There is a word, or two, left to be spoken
—Yet who would hear it ?   When so swiftly distance
Outmeasures time, engulfs identity ?

Already like the dreamer startled from sleep
And the vivid image lost even in waking,
There is no taste now for the shrunken sense to keep,
And these, the dreamer's eyes, are not alive to weep,
And this, the clinic heart, the dreamer's, is not breaking.

Is it so easy, then ?   Goodbye no more than this
Quiet disaster ?   And is there cause for sorrow
That in the small white murder of one kiss
Are born two ghosts, two Hamlets, two soliloquies,
Two worlds apart, tomorrow ?

HELEN SPALDING

THE CONFIRMATION

Yes, yours, my love, is the right human face.
I in my mind had waited for this long,
Seeing the false and searching for the true,
Then found you as a traveller finds a place
Of welcome suddenly amid the wrong
Valleys and rocks and twisting roads. But you,
What shall I call you? A fountain in a waste,
A well of water in a country dry,
Or anything that's honest and good, an eye
That makes the whole world bright. Your open heart,
Simple with giving, gives the primal deed,
The first good world, the blossom, the blowing seed,
The hearth, the steadfast land, the wandering sea,
Not beautiful or rare in every part,
But like yourself, as they were meant to be.

EDWIN MUIR

SONG

Warm are the still and lucky miles,
White shores of longing stretch away,
The light of recognition fills
    The whole great day, and bright
The tiny world of lovers' arms.

Silence invades the breathing wood
Where drowsy limbs a treasure keep,
Now greenly falls the learnèd shade
    Across the sleeping brows
And stirs their secret to a smile.

Restored! Returned! The lost are born
On seas of shipwreck home at last:
See! In the fire of praising burns
    The dry dumb past, and we
The life-day long shall part no more.

W. H. AUDEN

COWPER AT OLNEY

In this green valley where the Ouse
Is looped in many a silver pool,
Seeking God's mercy and his muse
Went Cowper sorrowful.

Like the pale gleam of wintry sun
His genius lit the obscure place,
Where, battling with despair, lived one
Of melancholy's race.

By quiet waters, by green fields
In winter sweet as summer hay,
By hedgerows where the chaffinch builds
He went his brooding way.

And not a berry or a leaf,
Or stirring bough or fragrant wind,
But, in its moment, soothed the grief
Of his tormented mind.

And since, like the belovèd sheep
Of David's shepherd, he was led
By streams and pastures quiet as sleep—
Was he not comforted?

SYLVIA LYND

WILLIAM WORDSWORTH

No room for mourning: he's gone out
Into the noisy glen, or stands between the stones
Of the gaunt ridge, or you'll hear his shout
Rolling among the screes, he being a boy again.
He'll never fail nor die,
And if they laid his bones
In the wet vaults or iron sarcophagi
Of fame, he'd rise at the first summer rain
And stride across the hills to seek
His rest among the broken lands and clouds.
He was a stormy day, a granite peak
Spearing the sky; and look, about its base
Words flower like crocuses in the hanging woods,
Blank though the dalehead and the bony face.

SIDNEY KEYES

I TAKE THEE, LIFE

I take thee, Life,
Because I need,
A wanton love
My flesh to feed.

But still my soul
Insatiate
Cries out, cries out
For its true mate.

MARGOT RUDDOCK

IN THE STRANGE ISLE

In the strange isle,
In the green freckled wood and grassy glade,
Strangely the man, the panther and the shadow
Move by the well and the white stones.

Voices cry out in trees, and fingers beckon,
The wings of a million butterflies are sunlight eyes,
There is no sword
In the enchanted wood.

Branches bend over like a terror,
The sun is darkened,
The white wind and the sun and the curling wave
Cradle the coral shore and the tall forest.

Ceaseless the struggle in the twining circles,
The gulls, the doves, and the dark crows ;
The fangs of the lily bleed, and the lips
Of the rose are torn.

Trees crash at midnight unpredicted,
Voices cry out,
Naked he walks, and with no fear,
In the strange isle, the wise and gentle.

MICHAEL ROBERTS

THE END OF FEAR

When a man has cast out fear
All is indifferent, and dear.

When desire has fled away
Then the little mice can play.

Leaning against the cedar's bark,
Or on a bear's neck in the dark,

Or lying in the mighty grass,
He is saved from what he was.

He can lay his head upon
Another's bosom, or a stone,

And the stone is well beloved,
And the breast by love unmoved :

The flesh uncursed and the stone blest,
The breast a stone, the stone a breast.

RUTH PITTER

WEEPING WATER

Weeping water, leaping fire,
God and my grave are my desire.
With swarming strife and scanty joy,
Little ease and long annoy,
I am damned and drowned in rue—
With love then what have I to do ?

With chaste stillness, blessèd peace,
No annoy and utter ease,
Lulled in morning's lap I lie
And mend my sorrows in the sky.
I am redeemed and flown above—
Then what have I to do with love?

Heaven is stillness, motion hell,
When I stir not I am well.
Wake me not, for I would be
Laid where quiet waits on me.
Lovely boy, I know you lie:
Frown as you will, but pass me by.

RUTH PITTER

IDLENESS

God, you've so much to do,
To think of, watch and listen to,
That I will let all else go by
And lending ear and eye
Help you to watch how in the combe
Winds sweep dead leaves without a broom;
And rooks in the spring-reddened trees
Restore their villages,
Nest by dark nest
Swaying at rest on trees' frail unrest;
Or on this limestone wall,
Listening at ease, with you recall
How once these heavy stones
Swam in the seas as shells and bones;
And hear that owl snore in a tree
Till it grows dark enough for him to see;
In fact, will learn to shirk
No idleness that I may share your work.

ANDREW YOUNG

THE MOURNER

When all your bitter grief is gone,
With anger and rebellion done,
Think then, with your more even breath—
How lovely was the face of Death!
Say you remember her sweet face,
   The light the loveliness;
The smile that passed beyond this world,
   To rest no more on us:
That, knowing now how Death is loved—
You follow her, and stand reproved.

W. H. DAVIES

THE HEDGE-ROW STORY

When fields here lose their colour, when the wood
trailing a hoary wing turns home
to raven night, I reckon up the sum
of rustic evil and clay-spattered good.

I think of the innumerable slow lives whose history
differs a hair's breadth from the hedge-row story:
thorns in black competition, the roped glory
of gossamer, soon gone,
with berries dipped in blood.

When fields here lose the light, I fear the mystery
of men like trees, that tower but touch the sky
they cannot and are felled one by one,
I think of saint and scarecrow schooled to die;
their leafless victory stands, where nothing stood.

LILIAN BOWES-LYON

A TIME TO DANCE

For those who had the power
  of the forest fires that burn
Leaving their source in ashes
  to flush the sky with fire:
Those whom a famous urn
  could not contain, whose passion
Brimmed over the deep grave
  and dazzled epitaphs:
For all that have won us wings
  to clear the tops of grief,
My friend who within me laughs
  bids you dance and sing.

Some set out to explore
  earth's limit, and little recked if
Never their feet came near it
  outgrowing the need for glory:
Some aimed at a small objective
  but the fierce updraught of their spirit
Forced them to the stars.
  Are honoured in public who built
The dam that tamed a river;
  or holding the salient for hours
Against odds, cut off and killed,
  are remembered by one survivor.

All these. But most for those
  whom accident made great,
As a radiant chance encounter
  of cloud and sunlight grows
Immortal on the heart:
  whose gift was the sudden beauty
Of a passing moment, enriches
  the fulfilled eye for ever.
Their spirits float serene
  above time's roughest reaches,
But their seed is in us and over
  our lives they are evergreen.

C. DAY LEWIS

THE OLD GODS

Old gods and goddesses who have lived so long
Through time and never found eternity,
Fettered by wasting wood and hollowing hill,

You should have fled our ever-dying song,
The mound, the well, and the green trysting tree
They are forgotten, yet you linger still.

Goddess of caverned breast and channelled brow
And cheeks slow hollowed by millennial tears,
Forests of autumn fading in your eyes,

Eternity marvels at your counted years
And kingdoms lost in time, and wonders how
There could be thoughts so bountiful and wise

As yours beneath the ever-breaking bough,
And vast compassion curving like the skies.

EDWIN MUIR

THE MAN WITHOUT FAITH

A man without faith
Grows old before his years,
His world a wraith,
For whom the end nears
Like a winter mist
When the sun is cold
In the cold west.

His children about him
Are strangers, unknown ;
The love that begot them
Cooled and gone.

If he get riches
They turn to rust,
And he can do nothing
With a handful of dust.
Life's miracle fails him,
Life's rapture, life's breath;
He has done with living,
He has forestalled death.

RICHARD CHURCH

THE STATIONARY JOURNEY

Here at my earthly station set,
  The revolutions of the year
Beat me bound and only let
  This astronomic world appear.

Yet if I could reverse my course
  Through ever-deepening yesterday,
Retrace the path that led me here,
  Could I find a different way?

I would see eld's frosted hair
  Burn black again and passion rage
On to its source and die away
  At last in childhood's tranquil age.

Charlemagne's death-palsied hand
  Would move once more and never rest
Until by deadlier weakness bound
  It lay against his mother's breast.

Saint Augustine gives back his soul
  To stumble in the endless maze,
After Jesus Venus stands
  In the full centre of his gaze,

While still from death to life to naught
  Gods, dynasties, and nations flit;
Though for a while among the sand
  Unchanged the changing Pharaohs sit.

Fast the horizons empty. Now
  Nothing's to see but wastes and rocks,
And on the thinning Asian plains
  A few wild shepherds with their flocks. . . .

So, back or forward, still we strike
  Through Time and touch its dreaded goal.
Eternity's the fatal flaw
  Through which run out world, life and soul.

And there in transmutation's blank
  No mortal mind has ever read,
Or told what soul and shape are, there,
  Blue wave, red rose, and Cæsar's head.

For there Immortal Being in
  Solidity more pure than stone
Sleeps through the circle, pillar, arch,
  Spiral, cone, and pentagon.

To the mind's eternity I turn,
  With leaf, fruit, blossom on the spray,
See the dead world grow green within
  Imagination's one long day.

There while outstretched upon the Tree
  Christ looks across Jerusalem's towers,
Adam and Eve unfallen yet
  Sleep side by side within their bowers.

There while fast in the Roman snare
  The Carthaginian thinks of home,
A boy carefree in Carthage streets,
  Hannibal fights a little Rome,

David and Homer tune their harps,
  Gaza is up, sprung from its wreck,
Samson goes free, Delilah's shears
  Join his strong ringlets to his neck.

A dream! the astronomic years
  Patrolled by stars and planets bring
Time led in chains from post to post
  Of the all-conquering Zodiac ring.

EDWIN MUIR

THE WALKING WOMAN

There's a hard wind yet and a sad road
Between the walking woman
And her deadly spouse, the iron lover.
O my hair has fallen and my man
Has fallen and my fruitful time is over:
There is a hard wind and a sad road.

There's a jangled verse, a cry
Beating behind that woman's face.
O my eyes are drowned and my man
Is drowned. Who loves a dead man's grace,
A drowned man's kisses or a blind man's eye?
Cries the unsatisfied, the walking woman.

There's all the angry air, the sea,
Between that woman and her hope:
O once I had a house, a fire
Until my man's proud faring broke
My house and heart. So I'll desire
Lovers of iron or dead men's constancy,
Cries the still passionate, the walking woman.

SIDNEY KEYES

WHAT THEN?

His chosen comrades thought at school
He must grow a famous man;
He thought the same and lived by rule,
All his twenties crammed with toil;
'What then?' sang Plato's ghost. 'What then?'

Everything he wrote was read,
After certain years he won
Sufficient money for his need,
Friends that have been friends indeed;
'What then?' sang Plato's ghost. 'What then?'

All his happier dreams came true—
A small old house, wife, daughter, son,
Grounds where plum and cabbage grew,
Poets and Wits about him drew;
'What then?' sang Plato's ghost. 'What then?'

'The work is done,' grown old he thought,
'According to my boyish plan;
Let the fools rage, I swerved in naught,
Something to perfection brought;'
But louder sang that ghost, 'What then?'

W. B. YEATS

HOSPITAL WARD (OF THIS GENERATION)

The world is sick, and we sick men
Listen for feet upon the stair:
And far off when we hear them, when,
Nigh to despair,
We think we hear them, we cry out
With hope and mockery and doubt
And blasphemy and prayer.

How beautiful the feet of them,
Thy messengers of peace!
But are they Thine? Shall they condemn,
Or bring release?
When all the thousand steps are climbed
At last, shall they appear
Haloed with life, or death-begrimed,
Hooded with fear?
In what strange guise to sick men's eyes
Shall they appear?

Far off the feet: along the ward
The sound-refusing doors are shut.
But through each window like a sword
The streams of sunshine cut;
And through each window, like a knife,
The blackbird's song,
The springtime of another life,
Does to the sick man wrong.
O light, to alien eyes unkind,
O light, to make the sick man blind,
O alien song, O song-bird's note
That clutches at the sick man's throat,
From company with you the years
Divide us, and our bitter tears.

The world is sick. Let not those feet
Delay upon the stairs:
For silence stabs, when their soft beat
Falls soundless on the air.

Have mercy on us sick, O Lord,
Who restless lie abed,
Praying and cursing in our ward,
And listening for their tread.

GEORGE ROSTREVOR HAMILTON

FÊTE CHAMPÊTRE

On the pavements the sexless toys run down.
Men and women go home to a sleep of stone.
The clock shows midnight only to the moon.

No dogs are barking, and no trains disturb
The dormitories of the new suburb.
The cat moves like a snowflake to the kerb.

The longest nightlight has long since burnt out
And somewhere else an unlatched garden gate
Strikes on the darkness of the dull and great.

The night is level on the hundred churches.
The human cry of the wind in the railway arches
Is conscience with his scolding images.

'The stallion is nameless, yet transmits his strength.
The childless hero dies in a bed at length.
Can you hold out till daylight in the glens?

'The ineffable has found its word again,
But not a bird cries, not a fabulous one,
But leaves you in the evenings more alone.

'There is not time for grief and less for love.
Loving is merely how the moments rave
Like the illusory movement of a wave.'

Though we are not as simple as we seem,
All men are simple in the act of dream;
To shudder and revoke the waking claim.

KENNETH ALLOTT

THE COCKY WALKERS

Grouped nightly at the cold, accepted wall,
Carved with a gaslight chisel the lean heads
Cry out unwittingly for Rembrandt's needle.
These are the flashy saplings whose domain
I cannot enter.
They burn at lip and fingertips the stuffed paper ;
The trouser-pocket boys, the cocky walkers,
Sons of old mothers, with their hats askew
Hummock the shoulder to the little flower
That lights the palm into a nightmare land,
A bloody basin of the sterile moon
That lights the face that sprouts the cigarette
Into a sudden passion of fierce colour.
Down the cold corridor of winter nights
I see a thousand groups that keep
The fag alight, at walls, and in the sharp
Stern corners of the street :
These are the sprigs ; flash boys, uncaught,
Treading the reedy springboard of green days.
Theirs is a headiness, for they
Have burned their lives up to the quarter-mark.
The days move by them and the chill nights hold them
In an old, unthought conspiracy, for they
Tinkle upon tin feet that send no root.
I see them at the cold, accepted wall,
The trouser-pocket boys, the cocky walkers.

MERVYN PEAKE

THIEF

To the galleys, thief, and sweat your soul out
With strong tugging under the curled whips,
That there your thievishness may find full play.
Whereas, before, you stole rings, flowers and watches,
Oaths, jests and proverbs,
Yet paid for bed and board like an honest man,
This shall be entire thiefdom : you shall steal
Sleep from chain-galling, diet from sour crusts,
Comradeship from the damned, the ten-year-chained—
And, more than this, the excuse for life itself
From a boat steered toward battles not your own.

ROBERT GRAVES

HATE

I hated a fellow-man long ago,
For he compassed my spirit's overthrow,
And the years that followed were bitter with woe.

And if someone had sent that man to his rest
I think that my heart would have danced in my breast,
And I dreamed that I sought him, and slew him with zest.

But a week gone by the word went round
That my enemy's body was under the ground ;
And my heart was heavy, and gave no sound.

Only the wind and the skies made call,
'God have pity upon you all.'

HERBERT PALMER

IN REGENT'S PARK

These Sunday mornings Londoners delight—
with or without the trotting child—
their workday eyes grown mild
but with their panoply precise and spry,
the handsome pleasure-ways of parks to try.

Dahlias down the banks flow crisp and bright,
the grass is winter-short and pungent,
dipping oars are plangent,
and in the light mist, dripping grey like silk,
water and trees and air seem smoothed in milk.

So that the forbidden island in the stream,
the chimney that over Lords looms,
and those peculiar domes,
might be near or distant illimitable miles;
and as the still sky breaks into a thousand gulls,

might burst into some bright or strange kind,
or open into a different scale.
To change in this style
is the property, I find, of love, which brings
a new dimension to all physical things.

For if I see my park with Vivian's eye—
the formal eye of a painter's mind—
it is changed as under his hand,
and through the mists of his being are visible
hints of glory before unimaginable.

One does not learn to look with another's eye
for ever, but the rigid world
moves and is unfurled.
This is the effect and virtue of passion's part,
that trains the eye and exercises the heart.

ANNE RIDLER

PRAYER FOR RAIN

O God, make it rain!
Loose the soft silver passion of the rain!
Send swiftly from above
This clear token of Thy love.
Make it rain!

Deck the bushes and the trees
With the tassels of the rain.
Make the brooks pound to the seas
And the earth shine young again.
God of passion, send the rain!

Oh, restore our ancient worth
With Thy rain!
Ease the heartache of the earth;
Sap the grain.
Fill the valleys and the dales
With Thy silver slanting gales;
And through England and wild Wales
Send the rain!

Lord, restore us to Thy will
With the rain!
Soak the valley, drench the hill,
Drown the stain;
Smite the mountain's withered hips,
Wash the rouge from sunset's lips,
Fill the sky with singing ships.
Send the rain!

HERBERT PALMER

SUMMER RAIN

Against the window pane,
against the temple of my brain
beat the muffled taps of rain.

Upon the scorched and mottled leaves,
upon the blenched and pented sheaves
the land receives

the liquid flood :
water like a blush of blood
returns to the parched rood.

The fox has left his fetid hovel
to lick the drenched blades of sorrel ;
odours rise from thyme and fennel.

The worm in his retreat deep under
the earth's insipid crust,
hearing a distant drumming thunder

blindly renews his upward undulation.
The soil respires as if in emulation
of living things. All elements their maculation

desire and achieve. A warm breath
issues from the nostrils beneath
the mask of death.

HERBERT READ

SONG

Nothing I have is worth a tear,
Books and papers, gauds and gear.
Happier beetle spread on his back
Than I boxed up with this what-d'ye-lack.
        What makes man as he stands ?
        Head, belly and hands,
Three to serve one, and the world goes on.

Once I'd a heart, but they did not approve it,
Slit up my side, and let remove it,
Since I've been good they have given to me
Paper galore, and much good may it do me.
    What brings man relief?
    Bread, pudding and beef.
Three kinds of food : paper's no good.

Soldiers tell me fighting's no frolic,
Wise men tell me love is a colic,
Bishops tell me learning's a lie—
Somebody tells me that I must die.
    What shall serve man then?
    Sword, sonnet or pen?
All things must fall ; God help us all!

E. N. DA COSTA ANDRADE

IN THESE OUR WINTER DAYS

In these our winter days
Death's iron tongue is glib
Numbing with fear all flesh upon
A fiery-hearted globe.

An age once green is buried,
Numbered the hours of light ;
Blood-red across the snow our sun
Still trails his faint retreat.

Spring through death's iron guard
Her million blades shall thrust ;
Love that was sleeping, not extinct,
Throw off the nightmare crust.

Eyes, though not ours, shall see
Sky-high a signal flame,
The sun returned to power above
A world, but not the same.

CECIL DAY LEWIS

AND DEATH SHALL HAVE NO DOMINION

And death shall have no dominion.
Dead men naked they shall be one
With the man in the wind and the west moon;
When their bones are picked clean and the clean bones gone,
They shall have stars at elbow and foot;
Though they go mad they shall be sane,
Though they sink through the sea they shall rise again;
Though lovers be lost love shall not;
And death shall have no dominion.

And death shall have no dominion.
Under the windings of the sea
They lying long shall not die windily;
Twisting on racks when sinews give way,
Strapped to a wheel, yet they shall not break;
Faith in their hands shall snap in two,
And the unicorn evils run them through;
Split all ends up they shan't crack;
And death shall have no dominion.

And death shall have no dominion.
No more may gulls cry at their ears
Or waves break loud on the seashores;
Where blew a flower may a flower no more
Lift its head to the blows of the rain;
Though they be mad and dead as nails,
Heads of the characters hammer through daisies;
Break in the sun till the sun breaks down,
And death shall have no dominion.

DYLAN THOMAS

TEMPT ME NO MORE

Tempt me no more ; for I
Have known the lightning's hour,
The poet's inward pride,
The certainty of power.

Bayonets are closing round.
I shrink : yet I must wring
A living from despair
And out of steel a song.

Though song, though breath be short,
I'll share not the disgrace
Of those that ran away
Or never left the base.

Comrades, my tongue can speak
No comfortable words,
Calls to a forlorn hope,
Gives work and not rewards.

Oh, keep the sickle sharp
And follow still the plough :
Others may reap, though some
See not the winter through.

Father, who endest all,
Pity our broken sleep ;
For we lie down with tears
And waken but to weep.

And if our blood alone
Will melt this iron earth,
Take it. It is well spent
Easing a saviour's birth.

CECIL DAY LEWIS

'NATION SHALL SPEAK PEACE . . .'

There are no frontiers in the air ;
Alien music, alien song,
Alien words are everywhere
On the silence borne along.

By the lifting of a hand
Voices from the sky come down ;
Songs we cannot understand
Yet would cherish as our own.

And these unknown hands which play ;
Unknown voices which can bless ;
Shall we at some blind hour slay
And forget their loveliness ?

Overhead an iron bird
Churns the air with channering noise ;
But the music is unstirred
And unstirred the singing voice.

WILLIAM SOUTAR

THE HAND THAT SIGNED THE PAPER FELLED A CITY

The hand that signed the paper felled a city ;
Five sovereign fingers taxed the breath,
Doubled the globe of dead and halved a country ;
These five kings did a king to death.

The mighty hand leads to a sloping shoulder,
The finger joints are cramped with chalk ;
A goose's quill has put an end to murder
That put an end to talk.

The hand that signed the treaty bred a fever,
And famine grew, and locusts came ;
Great is the hand that holds dominion over
Man by a scribbled name.

The five kings count the dead but do not soften
The crusted wound nor pat the brow ;
A hand rules pity as a hand rules heaven ;
Hands have no tears to flow.

DYLAN THOMAS

AS I WALKED OUT ONE EVENING

As I walked out one evening,
Walking down Bristol Street,
The crowds upon the pavement
Were fields of harvest wheat.

And down by the brimming river
I heard a lover sing
Under an arch of the railway
'Love has no ending.

'I'll love you, dear, I'll love you
Till China and Africa meet
And the river jumps over the mountain
And the salmon sing in the street.

'I'll love you till the ocean
Is folded and hung up to dry
And the seven stars go squawking
Like geese about the sky.

'The years shall run like rabbits,
For in my arms I hold
The Flower of the Ages
And the first love of the world.'

But all the clocks in the city
Began to whirr and chime:
'O let not Time deceive you,
You cannot conquer Time.

'In the burrows of the nightmare
Where Justice naked is,
Time watches from the shadow
And coughs when you would kiss.

'In headaches and in worry
Vaguely life leaks away,
And Time will have his fancy
To-morrow or to-day.

'Into many a green valley
Drifts the appalling snow;
Time breaks the threaded dances
And the diver's brilliant bow.

'O plunge your hands in water,
Plunge them in up to the wrist;
Stare, stare in the basin
And wonder what you've missed.

'The glacier knocks in the cupboard,
The desert sighs in the bed,
And the crack in the tea-cup opens
A lane to the land of the dead.

'Where the beggars raffle the banknotes
And the Giant is enchanting to Jack,
And the Lily-white Boy is a Roarer
And Jill goes down on her back.

'O look, look in the mirror,
O look in your distress;
Life remains a blessing
Although you cannot bless.

'O stand, stand at the window
As the tears scald and start;
You shall love your crooked neighbour
With your crooked heart.'

It was late, late in the evening,
The lovers they were gone;
The clocks had ceased their chiming
And the deep river ran on.

W. H. AUDEN

THE SNOW

In no way that I chose to go
Could I escape the falling snow.

I shut my eyes, wet with my fears ;
The snow still whispered in my ears.

I stopped my ears in deaf disguise :
The snow still fell before my eyes.

Snow was my comrade, snow my fate,
In a country huge and desolate.

My footsteps made a shallow space,
And then the snow filled up the place,

And all the walking I had done
Was on a journey not begun.

I did not know the distance gone,
But resolutely travelled on,

While silently on every hand
Fell the sorrow of the land,

And no way that I chose to go
Could lead me from the grief of snow.

CLIFFORD DYMENT

THE AXE IN THE WOOD

I stopped to watch a man strike at the trunk
Of a tree grown strong through many centuries.
His quick axe, sharp and glittering, struck deep,
And yellow chips went spinning in the air—

And I remember how I liked the sight
Of poise and rhythm as the bright axe swung.
A man who fells a tree makes people watch,
For glory seems to crowd upon the axe.

I know the answers to the chance reproach:
How old the tree was, and how dangerous,
How it might fall, how timber in a stack
Had more good in it than a growing tree—
But I saw death cut down a thousand men
In that tall lovely legacy of wood.

CLIFFORD DYMENT

STRANGERS

The sad bells sound;
Night hastens on apace;
Oh, leave me not to languish
    In this place!

I stand—I know—
Beside you, weeping not,
Pressing my childish Why?
    My stubborn What?

I would forgive
If only a dream you are,
If only a little I'm to stay,
    And wake afar.

Cold is this church,
Cold the high arches, cold,
With dazzling light, and Oh,
    How old! how old!

Under the hollow roof
The strangers' voices come—
'The night is dark, and I
    Am far from home.'

WALTER DE LA MARE

WHAT WAS LOST

I sing what was lost and dread what was won,
I walk in a battle fought over again,
My king a lost king, and lost soldiers my men;
Feet to the Rising and Setting may run,
They always beat on the same small stone.

W. B. YEATS

THE WRONG ROAD

Say this when you return,
'I came by the wrong road,
And saw the starved woods burn.
I stopped, bewildered, lost,
And of a sudden, heard
The red-throated bird,
The holy bird, the ghost.
I felt the shivering reed
Fevered with frost.
I watched the Crucified
Writhing upon the Cross
With the spear in His side,
And beneath Him the moss
With the crimson buds
Tortured, multiplied
Under the dripping goad,
Close by the road,
The wrong road.'

RICHARD CHURCH

POEM

Heart of the heartless world,
Dear heart, the thought of you
Is the pain at my side,
The shadow that chills my view.

The wind rises in the evening
Reminds that autumn is near.
I am afraid to lose you,
I am afraid of my fear.

On the last mile to Huesca,
The last fence for our pride,
Think so kindly, dear, that I
Sense you at my side.

And if bad luck should lay my strength
Into the shallow grave,
Remember all the good you can;
Don't forget my love.

JOHN CORNFORD

ONE NIGHT

One night he lay on my breast,
One rapt swift-fleeting night;
Then marched away with the rest
In the morning light:
For I was only a woman, and so
I had to let him go.

And now another's breast
Holds him through endless night;
And he marches no more with the rest
In the morning light:
For she is his mother, the earth, and so
Need never let him go.

WILFRID GIBSON

THREE CITIES

Crossing the border, the first city I came to
Was white with death.
  No orders harsh, no living voices rude,
  Jarred the equality and quietude
Of citizens with feet to the sunset lying.

Crossing the border, the next city I came to
Was grey with sleep.
  I heard men breathe, I heard a watchman shout,
  I heard a soul in frenzy of dream cry out,
And citizens in rooms unquiet stirring.

Crossing the border, the third city I came to
Was red with life.
  They worked, they fed, they lived, in equal shares,
  They marched in line, they wheeled, they formed in squares,
The citizens for war to the death preparing.

GEORGE ROSTREVOR HAMILTON

LULLABY

Though the world has slipped and gone,
Sounds my loud discordant cry
Like the steel bird's song on high:
'Still one thing is left—the Bone!'
Then outdanced the Babioun.

She sat in the hollow of the sea—
A socket whence the eye's put out—
She sang to the child a lullaby
(The steel birds' nest was thereabout).

'Do, do, do, do—
Thy mother's hied to the vaster race:
The Pterodactyl made its nest
And laid a steel egg in her breast—
She'll work no more, nor dance, nor moan,
And I am come to take her place,
Do, do.

'There's nothing left but earth's low bed—
(The Pterodactyl fouls its nest) :
But steel wings fan thee to thy rest,
And wingless truth and larvae lie
And eyeless hope and handless fear—
All these for thee as toys are spread,
Do—do—

'Red is the bed of Poland, Spain,
And thy mother's breast, who has grown wise
In that fouled nest. If she could rise,
Give birth again,

'In wolfish pelt she'd hide thy bones
To shield thee from the world's long cold,
And down on all fours shouldst thou crawl,
For thus from no height canst thou fall—
Do, do.

'She'd give no hands : there's naught to hold
And naught to make : there's dust to sift,
But no food for the hands to lift.
Do, do.

'Heed my ragged lullaby,
Fear not living, fear not chance ;
All is equal—blindness, sight,
There is no depth, there is no height :
Do, do.

'The Judas-coloured sun is gone,
And with the Ape thou art alone—
Do,
Do.'

EDITH SITWELL

CLASSIC ENCOUNTER

Arrived upon the downs of asphodel
I walked towards the military quarter
To find the sunburnt ghosts of allied soldiers
Killed on the Chersonese.

I met a band of palefaced weary men
Got up in odd equipment. 'Hi,' I said,
'Are you Gallipoli?'

And one, the leader, with a voice of gold,
Answered: 'No. Ours, Sir, was an older bungle.
We are Athenian hoplites who sat down
Before young Syracuse.

'Need I recount our too-much-memoired end?
The hesitancy of our General Staff,
The battle in the Harbour, where Hope fled
But we could not?

'Not our disgrace in that,' the leader added,
'But we are those proficient in the arts
Freed in return for the repeated verses
Of our Euripides.

'Those honeyed words did not soothe Cerberus'
(The leader grinned), 'For sulky Charon hire
Deficient, and by Rhadamanthos ruled
No mitigation.

'And yet with men, born victims of their ears,
The chorus of the weeping Troades
Prevailed to gain the freedom of our limbs
And waft us back to Athens.

'Through every corridor of this old barracks
We wander without friends; not fallen or
Survivors in a military sense:
Hence our disgrace.'

He turned; and as the rank mists took them in
They chanted of the God to Whom men pray,
Whether He be Compulsion, or All-Fathering,
Or Fate and blind.

CHRISTOPHER CAUDWELL

IN TIME OF SUSPENSE

Draw-to the curtains then, and let it rain.
We'll look no more on that disordered scene:
Blind rage upon a blinded window-pane,
The shivering white upon the darkening green;
Nor that beyond it leaping to and fro,
Ghost in the ruined garden, or mad briar.
Shut out confusion, draw the curtains to,
Build the cathedrals of the fire anew.
Close, eyes, on doubt, and open on desire.

Here, in the quiet brilliance of belief,
We fashion life at such intensity,
The very chairs might rustle into leaf
And panels grope to build their primal tree.
Now when our bodies meet like star and star,
Now when our minds remoter commerce do,
No wish too subtle and no world too far,
But we, so perfectly in tune we are,
Passionately conceive and make it true.

And so farewell to Winter; for I hear
The lambs rejoicing on a hill of jade,
The blackbird in his vocal graph of fear
Scattering darkness down the painted glade.
It crowds the curtains, mad in bud and wing,
That world of passion that your fancy craves,
That England that the fancy, quickening,
Cannot but call the very eye of Spring,
Lashed by the curled abandon of her waves!

Folly of dreaming, when you have entwined
Wild arms about the dreamer and the dream!
Drawn by those gentle Avons I shall find
A land where April does not merely seem.
Narrow horizons! Yet how wide to me
For whom they compass all those island charms
That I must die to safeguard, it may be:
An England the aspiring candles see,
Narrow enough to compass in my arms.

So in this room. But when I stood alone
One evening on a windy crown of land
Beneath the emblem of a youthful moon,
And watched oblivion like a tired hand
Folding the map of Spring away, I knew
Hill upon hill receding were no more
Than picture and faint effigy of you,
Nor shall I ever after lose that view
Though I descend into the night of war.

For us, no heartening slogan will assuage
What must be suffered in the mad descent.
We dreamed that war was but an awkward age
And country could be lost in continent.
The cretin world remains where it began,
Clings to the shambles and improvement shelves.
Too undeceived for patriotic man
Youth takes up arms to rescue what it can;
For all is lost but what we have ourselves.

When war came to our cradles once, it meant
Only the mutter of a thunder-clap
Somewhere beyond the tidy hills of Kent,
A black line every morning on a map,
Germans in the allotment, trains unlit—
Did we not learn of war in gentle doses?
We merely breathed it like a dangerous grit
In every breath we drew, contracted it
From our warm bottles, like tuberculosis.

Formed by the years of agony, wherein
Fear stole into the heart and set up house,
Formed to be nervous as a violin,
We find no brothers in the dead. For us
No voice will speak in the white cemeteries
Of France. We are not of that careless kind
To whom life seemed to offer prize on prize,
Who, at the terminus, with laughing eyes
Saw only joy in battle. Blind, stark blind.

Nor are we of the next unhappy age
That laughed, with laughter hollow as an urn
Raised to Belief, the murdered heritage.
Now from those ageing pantaloons we learn
The young are very serious. Even so.
As passionately serious as the Spring
After the sterile gaieties of snow.
Give us but time enough, and we will show
These barren valleys how to laugh and sing!

Give us but time, we say. For now, on all,
The radiant anguish of a dream is thrown.
Vivid the bird beyond the orchard wall
Who fills Goodnight with poignancy unknown.
More beautiful because it is more haunted
Our world revolves. Accusing as a text,
These walls, these shapes of love we have been granted,
Are critically watching though enchanted:
'This Winter, yes,' they nod at us. 'But next?'

Thus for the island genius, Liberty,
Much loved by Roman letters in our stone,
Another generation learns to die
Gravely, not caring if the flags are flown,
Believing simply it must save for Earth
A way of life becoming to mankind,
A grace of centuries, a thing of worth:
This we believe, who by a peaceful hearth
Have laughing eyes tonight, but are not blind.

Then let the violin on its own nerves
Be racked, if only the sweet Master seek
The harmony its brittle heart conserves.
What if, while you and I contrive to speak
With exiled April in a distant room,
The clouds should lift, and a young moon outside
Swim like an amulet beyond the gloom?
Shall we not look upon this night to come?
Blow out the candles—throw the curtains wide!

LAWRENCE WHISTLER

FLIGHT

By day, the returning terror of swifts, the scream
Of the loop over leaf, the power-dive on to the thatch;
And the robin whose vivid gift is a tongue of flame
To startle the stone at your foot into lyrical speech.
By night the approach of the bat, neurotic and odd,
A flicker of bony fingers here and there;
And the cool owl swimming in the blinded wood,
A big moth saying nothing in grey air.

By day, the shuttle of colour, speed that belongs,
To the shadow that drops like a stone, the jewel that soars.
By night, the suspicion, the mere innuendo of wings,
The hint of a fugitive shadow across the stars.

By day, *Jubilate* of saints in the heart of the holly,
By night, the cry of the lost in the luminous valley.

LAWRENCE WHISTLER

THE KESTRELS

When I would think of you, my mind holds only
The small defiant kestrels—how they cut
The raincloud with sharp wings, continually circling
About a storm-rocked elm, with passionate cries.
It was an early month. The plow cut hard.
The may was knobbed with chilly buds. My folly
Was great enough to lull away my pride.

There is no virtue now in blind reliance
On place or person or the forms of love.
The storm bears down the pivotal tree, the cloud
Turns to the net of an inhuman fowler
And drags us from the air. Our wings are clipped.
Yet still our love and luck lies in our parting:
Those cries and wings surprise our surest act.

SIDNEY KEYES

REFLECTIONS ON THE FALL OF FRANCE, JUNE 1940

Under these brooding skies,
Still, pewter-grey,
Why is it, France, of you
I've dreamed all day?
On the dark fountain's face
Fall the bright leaves;
Memory's looking glass
Where the heart grieves.

Here are tall forest trees,
Half-dreamt, half-known,
Brown as old tapestries,
Their summer flown;
Here one of Corot's ponds
Hidden, remote,
Where a small red-capped boy
Tethers his goat.

Silent these autumn woods;
Then faint, forlorn,
From some deep castled glade
Sounds the sad horn;
Echoes of cavalcades
Ridden away,
Magic of poets' words
Time can't betray:

Words sown so long ago
In an old lamplit room
Where a dear Mademoiselle
Taught them to bloom.
France, it's not true today,
True that you're gone!
You who are part of us,
Bone of our bone!

EILUNED LEWIS

WAITING FOR THE WIND

The year turns. Summer blown from Europe
fills skies with grazing islands, throws sickle beaches
flecked with red feathers round uncharted bays

only a day ago I saw a cloud
grey as burnt straw, shaped like an ear of wheat
lie tall across the country, from sky to sky

preceding wind, a banner. Here in England
how we lie silent watching the bowl of sky
how we lie silent waiting for the wind—

millions listening for it, for the clicking of twigs
or patter of leaves before it, say under their breath
'Now it is bending the spruces northward on Europe

gathering resin and thunder. Yesterday I saw
a hairy cloud, a banner being carried
over the roofs of London, white at mid-day

but by night a red veil on the sun.'
Millions expecting the sudden running of news—
'It has crossed the coast: eastward the dunes are smoking.'

Only a day ago I saw a cloud
feathered like pride, a banner high over Essex
but no lathe stopped to watch it hasten

no flier under it saw the streets
mile upon mile of rearing faces, figures
running into the fields and staring upwards—

light and white as ash of straws, a banner
shaped like an ear of wheat, full of small breasts
and after it the quick invincible wind.

But still the talk runs, mouth to ear, 'the wind
is coming, is crossing the coast.' In the fields no noise
as yet, but the starlings telling of weather.

ALEX COMFORT

HIGH FLIGHT

Oh! I have slipped the surly bonds of earth
  And danced the skies on laughter-silvered wings;
Sunward I've climbed, and joined the tumbling mirth
  Of sun-split clouds—and done a hundred things
You have not dreamed of—wheeled and soared and swung
  High in the sunlit silence. Hov'ring there
I've chased the shouting wind along, and flung
  My eager craft thro' footless halls of air.

Up, up the long, delirious, burning blue
  I've topped the wind-swept heights with easy grace
Where never lark, nor even eagle flew—
  And while with silent, lifting mind I've trod
The high, untrespassed sanctity of space,
  Put out my hand and touched the face of God.

JOHN GILLESPIE MAGEE

I THINK CONTINUALLY

I think continually of those who were truly great,
Who, from the womb, remembered the soul's history
Through corridors of light where the hours are suns
Endless and singing. Whose lovely ambition
Was that their lips, still touched with fire,
Should tell of the Spirit clothed from head to foot in song.
And who hoarded from the Spring branches
The desires falling across their bodies like blossoms.

What is precious is never to forget
The essential delight of the blood drawn from ageless springs
Breaking through rocks in worlds before our earth.
Never to deny its pleasure in the morning simple light
Nor its grave evening demand for love.
Never to allow gradually the traffic to smother
With noise and fog the flowering of the spirit.

Near the snow, near the sun, in the highest fields
See how these names are fêted by the waving grass
And by the streamers of white cloud
And whispers of wind in the listening sky.
The names of those who in their lives fought for life,
Who wore at their hearts the fire's centre.
Born of the sun they travelled a short while towards the sun,
And left the vivid air signed with their honour.

STEPHEN SPENDER

STILL FALLS THE RAIN

(THE RAIDS, 1940. NIGHT AND DAWN)

Still falls the Rain—
Dark as the world of man, black as our loss—
Blind as the nineteen hundred and forty nails
Upon the Cross.

Still falls the Rain
With a sound like the pulse of the heart that is changed to the
hammer-beat
In the Potter's Field, and the sound of the impious feet

On the Tomb :
Still falls the Rain
In the Field of Blood where the small hopes breed and the
human brain
Nurtures its greed, that worm with the brow of Cain.

Still falls the Rain
At the feet of the Starved Man hung upon the Cross.
Christ that each day, each night, nails there, have mercy on
us—
On Dives and on Lazarus :
Under the Rain the sore and the gold are as one.

Still falls the Rain—
Still falls the Blood from the Starved Man's wounded Side:
He bears in His Heart all wounds,—those of the light that died,

The last faint spark
In the self-murdered heart, the wounds of the sad uncomprehending dark,
The wounds of the baited bear,—
The blind and weeping bear whom the keepers beat
On his helpless flesh . . . the tears of the hunted hare.

Still falls the Rain—
Then—O Ile leape up to my God: who pulles me doune—
See, see where Christ's blood streames in the firmament:
It flows from the Brow we nailed upon the tree
Deep to the dying, to the thirsting heart
That holds the fires of the world,—dark-smirched with pain
As Cæsar's laurel crown.

Then sounds the voice of One who like the heart of man
Was once a child who among beasts has lain—
'Still do I love, still shed my innocent light, my Blood, for thee.'

EDITH SITWELL

LONDON

London, the 'Flower of Cities All'—
As old Dunbar once did you call—
'Rose Royal and Original!'

You, that have seen beneath your sky
Long lines of men go marching by
To take the field for Liberty!

What threat of War and War's deray
Hath shook your walls that yesterday
Heard merry-make and pipers play?

What sable pall is dropt by night
Upon the town that shone so bright,
Streets, shops ashine, and myriad light?

And they, your peerless women, they
That are your silent soldiery—
What fate for them, and theirs, may be?

And we that are your sons of grace—
This night we bow like one that prays,
For a man must love his mothering-place.

And when the war-planes hover near,
And the wing'd harpies swoop and lower,
We love you most, O fadeless flower.

ERNEST RHYS

THE CHILDREN

Upon the street they lie
Beside the broken stone:
The blood of children stares from the broken stone.

Death came out of the sky
In the bright afternoon:
Darkness slanted over the bright afternoon.

Again the sky is clear
But upon earth a stain:
The earth is darkened with a darkening stain:

A wound which everywhere
Corrupts the hearts of men:
The blood of children corrupts the hearts of men.

Silence is in the air:
The stars move to their places:
Silent and serene the stars move to their places:

But from the earth the children stare
With blind and fearful faces:
And our charity is in the children's faces.

WILLIAM SOUTAR

A HOUSE IN WARTIME

Look at this ancient house; it has survived
Three centuries of time, and human history.
Things have grown old in it. Grandfather clocks
Have frayed much catgut hauling down the hours,
Pot handles have worn smooth, and poker-knobs
Been polished by palms long folded over breasts
Now quiet and untroubled in the churchyard.

Search any corner here, attic or cellar,
Odd pantry cupboard or a gunroom shelf,
You'll find the throw-outs of ten generations,
Household rubbish made romantic by time;
Print bonnets, bundles of letters, broken toys,
Pathetic vestiges of civilized life,
Emblems of peace and a continued growth
In one place, in one faith, of civil man
And all his works. Here is the centre of it,
That long activity in hope; the plans,
The achievement, the discarded and replaced,
All gathered in this house, beneath a roof
Where the bats hang, and hermit spiders lurk.
I should be sure enough of all I hold
Within such walls. I should look out through windows
Set three feet back in mellowed brick and stone,
And stand secure amid my universe
Now turning to its rich, late summer days,
Life's discipline grown fruitful. I should see,
Like some old patriarch in a lost religion,
My wife and children round me, the fulfilment
Of mutual love beyond the need of words.

Instead I hear the wind wail in the walls.
By night and day I hear the fleets of death
Pass overhead, to deal out mutilation
On those who have no quarrel with the sky,
But look to it as their forefathers looked,
For rain, for sunshine, for the busy song
Of larks in spring, and movement of the stars,
Those symbols of a God half-understood.

The ancient house dissolves. My lifework thins
And a reverberation tears it down.
My gathered harvest is consumed in fire,
Thunder, and fire that flashes in their eyes,
My loved ones, gone down in their agony.
The raid is done. The sky is clear again
For stars by night, and singing lark by day.
Eternity once more puts on the mask
Of time, to hide its dreadful wisdom from me.

Still, after peril, stands my house foursquare,
Still, with the nightmare passed, I may contrive
To comfort those I yet may call my own.
The clock ticks on, the bat and spider keep
A sacred shadow in the roof above.
Laughter, love's fullest echo, fills the house.
Nothing has changed, except that Universe
I dared to raise, before I looked on fear.

RICHARD CHURCH

LETTER TO MY WIFE

The loud mechanical voices of the sirens
Lure me from sleep, and on the heath, like stars,
Moths fall into a mounting shaft of light.
Airplanes whirr over and then the night stays quiet;
The moon is peeled of cloud, its gold is changed
On stone for silver and the cap of sky
Glitters like quartz, impersonal and remote.
This surface is the same, the clock's bland face,
Its smiling moustaches, hide the spring, knotted
Like muscles, and the crouching jungle hammer.

The same but so different with you not here.
This evening when I turned from the clothes you left,
Empty and silk, the souls of swallows flickered
Against the glass of our house: I felt no better
Along the tree-massed alleys where I saw
The long pale legs on benches in the dark.

It was no vague nostalgia which I breathed
Between the purple colloids of the air;
My lust was as precise and fierce as that of
The wedge-headed jaguar or the travelling Flaubert.

But I only encountered the ghosts of the suburb,
Those ghosts you know and who are real and walk
And talk in the small public gardens, by the tawdry
Local monuments; the Witch and Big Head
And the others, fleeting and familiar as
Our memories and ambitions, and just as dead.
Being alone they stopped me; Big Head first.
Removing her unbelievable hat, she showed me
What before I had only conjectured, and she whispered:
O lucky you—you might have been born like this.

I knew it was true but, hurrying on, the Witch
Lifted her cane and barred the way: she is
Lean and very dirty, but hanging round
That skeleton are rags of flesh still handsome.
Moving her lips madly and in a foreign tone she said:
Oh, do not hope, boy—you will come to this.
I ran, being certain that she had not erred,
Back to our room where now the only noise
Is the icy modulated voice of Mozart
And the false clock ticking on the mantelpiece.

Now in the bubble of London whose glass will soon
Smear into death, at the still calm hour of four,
I see the shadows of our life, the Fates
We narrowly missed, our possible destiny.
I try to say that love is more solid than
Our bodies, but I only want you here.
I know they created love and that the rest
Is ghosts; war murders love—I really say
But dare I write it to you who have said it
Always and have no consolation from the ghosts?

ROY FULLER

THE CRUEL SOLSTICE

To-night the stranger city and the old
Moon that stands over it, proclaim
A cruel solstice, coming ice and cold
Thoughts and the darkening of the heart's flame.

'Stand up,' speaks soul, 'let wisdom turn the time
Into an image of your day's despite';
O clever soul, we were born separate,
Held only in hard glance or studied rhyme.

'Sleep then, tired singer, stop the mouth
Of the unhappy month and take your rest.'
O cunning voice, I have not strength enough,
Being no stranger here, but uncouth guest.

So must I walk or falter by the wall,
Wondering at my impotence
Of thought and action; at the fall
Of love and cities and the heart's false diligence.

To-night I cannot speak, remembering
For all my daily talk, I dare not enter
The empty month; can only stand and think
Of you, my dearest, and the approaching winter.

SIDNEY KEYES

TO MY WIFE

Out of the wind and the wind's image
tall and impatient as a moving tree,
you run as you will run age after age
as bright in beauty as the mind can see:
moving within the wind, within the mind,
carried away, away with waving hair
wind-ruffed, waving as you leave behind
the mortal picture Time will seek to draw:
and yet that Time will never quite impair,
for the wind's image like a moving wand
will draw this single tree against your hair,
and its gold leaf will linger in the mind
when the wind drops and Time and tree are bare.

JOHN BAYLISS

TAKE YOUR GUN

Man, take your gun : and put to shame
earthquake and plague, the acts of God.
You maim the crazy and the lame.

Terror is their palsy, the knees
of men buckle for fear of man.
You are the God whom frenzy pleases.

You are the gas-man, and the flier
who drops his bomb ; the man in tanks.
You wire mines and fear the fire.

And dig the hollow street with trenches
the gas-main and the sewer cross.
The stench of dead men makes you flinch.

But if the dying whimper, pain
pricks you like courage, like delight.
The vein sings to the cruel brain.

What are you, man, that gun in hand
with savagery and pity go,
and face to face with madness stand ;

and acid-drenched and poison-sprayed
see flame run lovely like a wake
from raiders ; and the burning lake
shake overhead ? You are afraid.

The shadow flickers on the wall
like morse, like gun-shot. Terror walks
the tall roofs where the snipers hawk.
He stalks you, man. And, man, you fall.

J. BRONOWSKI

'NO CLOCK WITH NUMBERED EYES'

No clock with numbered eyes or measured bell
Sparely across the dark to give us word
Of the lost sun's huge whereabouts, no starred
And wheeling roof of air whose patterns tell
The hour—but like that medieval hell
Preached of in choirs where now the heron perches
Grey among skeleton windows, these night watches,
Moonless and full of poignant waiting, still
Proffer no light nor clue for guessing. Dusk
Once black, somewhere there's morning on the march;
Two years away, or three, or not so much?
And how's the sky? Will morning be the husk
Of our desire, or passionate, frosty-keen,
To shake us out of death and wash us clean?

CHRISTOPHER HASSALL

THE ONLY PRETTY RINGTIME

Stern Lover in your helm of steel,
What dreadful tryst is this you keep?
The birds in heav'n now drone of death . . .
A lover must still hold his breath,
Nor lose the power to think and feel.

For love no longer swoons on sleep,
But wide-eyed waits, forsworn to save:
Now any time hell's din may start,
And shot and shell make great the heart,
While fires of death more fiercely leap!

Still, still victorious o'er the grave
Shall walk the lover and his lass,
Spring strow her flowers with healing hands
Above the hurt and haggard lands,
And blunt the blades with sheaves of grass.

A. V. BOWEN

THE INVADER

Our shops and farms wide open lie;
Still the invader feels a lack:
Disquiet whets his gluttony
For what he may not carry back.

He prowls about in search of wealth
But has no skill to recognize
Our things of worth: we need no stealth
To mask them from his pauper eyes.

He calls for worship and amaze;
We give him yes-men in a row,
Reverberating that self-praise
He wearied of a while ago.

He casts around for some new whim,
Something preposterously more:
'Love me' he bids. We offer him
The slack embraces of a whore.

And when he spitefully makes shift
To share with us his pauperdom,
By forcing on us as a gift
The shoddy wares he brought from home,

And watches that we sell and buy
Amongst us his degrading trash,
He gets no gain at all. Though sly
With what he knows, the guns and cash,

What he knows not he may not touch;
Those very spoils for which he came
Are still elusive to his clutch—
They swerve and scorch him like a flame.

Invader-outcast of all lands,
He lives condemned to gorge and crave,
To foul his feast with his own hands:
At once the oppressor and the slave.

NORMAN CAMERON

STREET SONG

'Love my heart for an hour, but my bone for a day—
At least the skeleton smiles, for it has a morrow:
But the hearts of the young are now the dark treasure of
Death,
And summer is lonely.

'Comfort the lonely light and the sun in its sorrow,
Come like the night, for terrible is the sun
As truth, and the dying light shows only the skeleton's hunger
For peace, under the flesh like the summer rose.

'Come through the darkness of death, as once through the
branches
Of youth you came, through the shade like the flowering door
That leads into Paradise, far from the street,—you, the unborn
City seen by the homeless, the night of the poor.

'You walk in the city ways, where Man's threatening shadow,
Red-edged by the sun like Cain, has a changing shape—
Elegant like the Skeleton, crouched like the Tiger,
With the age-old wisdom and aptness of the Ape.

'The pulse that beats in the heart is changed to the hammer
That sounds in the Potter's Field where they build a new
world
From our Bone, and the carrion-bird days' foul droppings
and clamour—
But you are my night, and my peace,—

'The holy night of conception, of rest, the consoling
Darkness when all men are equal,—the wrong and the right,
And the rich and the poor are no longer separate nations,—
They are brothers in night.'

This was the song I heard; but the Bone is silent!
Who knows if the sound was that of the dead light calling,—
Of Cæsar rolling onward his heart, that stone,
Or the burden of Atlas falling.

EDITH SITWELL

CRUCIFORM

Here, in the sand, where some one laid him down,
The one known human signature is clear.
Whether woman or man, white-skinned or brown,
Whether the outflung arms were so for fear
Or agony or weariness or shame,
Here, in one line athwart another line,
Is briefly written the one, mutual name,
A saviour's, or a thief's, or yours, or mine.
Dunes sifted undersea long since have borne
This self-same cross, small and anonymous ;
Tan deserts, that the wind has not yet worn,
Will print the symbol. And not one of us,
But then, or some day, could lie down and fit
Our desolate arms and bodies into it.

WINIFRED WELLES

TEARS

Temper, blood and speech divide
The nations jangling side by side ;
Nor can one close-bordering land
The other's laughter understand.

Yet have all the sons of Earth
One thing common from their birth ;
Stands alone through changing years
The catholicity of tears :

Whose eloquence at last may teach
And reconcile them each to each.

GEORGE ROSTREVOR HAMILTO

ECLOGUE

When all the powers have fallen
It will be late in autumn
And lovers then will wander
Between still trees and water,
Between the leaves' swoon
And the mirrored swan.
They will no more be startled
When all the guns have hurtled
Down precipice and panic,
But will put on the tunic
Of beauty and secureness
Knowing that no recurrence
Of the inherited hate
Will glaze their eyes with heat.
Grief was clean gone
Never to grow again
When she whose mortal sickness
Worsened with all physicians
Of love's garment laid hold
And by the hem was healed.
O thrice and four times blessed
Above the pitch of guessing
Who in the changed future
Will sense the cure of nature
And know their kind delivered
From the issue of blood forever.
   O that my eyes and yours
Before the drift of years
Defeat us in the tomb
Might see that lightsome time:
When shattered lies the piston
Rivet and rod unfastened,
Belt crank and lever broken,
Flywheel rusted in bracken.
Then would we walk and suffer
Bramble and brake to cover
Ruins of embassies
And splintered balconies,

See pools in sunlight gem
The roofless robing room,
Moonlight and ivy stencil
The place of the council.
We would not think, though hungry,
That rain and storm were angry
But would rejoice to endure
With the wild hare and deer
Frost whirlwind fire and lightning ;
And with the light latening
Our eyes would not be poor
Seeing the hours repair
With leaf and arrayed blossom,
As with a proved balsam,
The surgery of winter.
O then in peace would enter
Spring and highest summer,
Not in pride and armour.

HAL SUMMERS

THE TROPHY

The wise king dowered with blessings on his throne,
The rebel raising the flag in the market place,
Haunt me like figures on an ancient stone
The ponderous light of history beats upon,
Or the enigma of a single face
Handed unguessed, unread from father to son,
As if it dreamed within itself alone.

Regent and rebel clash in horror and blood
Here on the blindfold battlefield. But there,
Motionless in the grove of evil and good
They grow together and their roots are twined
In deep confederacy far from the air,
Sharing the secret trophy each with other ;
And king and rebel are like brother and brother,
Or father and son, co-princes of one mind,
Irreconcilables, their treaty signed.

EDWIN MUIR

SOWING SEED

As my hand dropt a seed
In the dibbled mould
And my mind hurried onward
To picture the miracle
June should unfold,

On a sudden before me
Hanging its head
With black petals
Rotting and tainted
Stood a flower, dead ;

As if all the world's hope
Were rotting there,
A thing to weep for,
Ripe for burial,
Veined with despair.

Yet I cannot prevent
My ignorant heart
From trust that is deeper
Than fear can fathom
Or hope desert.

The small twy-bladed
Shoot will thrust
To brave all hazards.
The seed is sown
And in Earth I trust.

LAURENCE BINYON

HISTORY

Time has stored all, but keeps his chronicle
In secret, beyond all our probe or gauge.
There flows the human story, vast and full;
And here a muddy trickle smears the page.

The things our hearts remember make a sound
So faint; so loud the menace and applause.
The gleaners come, with eyes upon the ground
After Oblivion's harvest, picking straws.

What is man, if this only has told his tale,
For whom ruin and blunder mark the years,
Whom continent-shadowing conquerors regale
To surfeiting, with glory of blood and tears?

He flaunts his folly and woe in a proud dress:
But writes no history of his happiness.

LAURENCE BINYON

SO STILL THE WORLD

(*from 'Winter Solstice'*)

So still the world this winter noon,
So sparkling-cold and still,
Of quietness the heart
Could take her fill.

Upon the shallow snow
Clear rang my careful tread.
Summer had died, long ago,
But was not dead,

While from the lattice thorn,
To chide my lingering doubt,
Lively with faith and fear
A feathered eye looked out,

And on the powdered verge,
Where road gives way to grass
For others' coming and going,
Many a printing was

Of blackbird, of wren:
Who burn away their blood,
Even as we,
To ends not understood.

So rare the fallen fleece of sky,
So far the noise of men,
Myself for a musing moment
Was blackbird, was wren.

GERALD BULLETT

SLEEP

The ring and rim
Of tidal sleep
Will slip and creep
Along my limbs

And I shall watch,
But never catch
The final change,
The water-plunge,

And through what caves
Beneath what waves
I then shall go
I shall not know,

For I shall come
From that lost land
Half-blind, half-dumb,
With, in my hand,

A fish's head,
A shell, a shred
Of seaweed and
Some grains of sand.

A. S. J. TESSIMOND

COUNTRY LIFE

The troubled man turned head away ;
  Heedless, he saw the river gliding,
The reeds of sword-steel, and the grey
  Reflected clouds fast riding ;
He saw the foam, the water's colour,
  The whirlpools dwindling as they ran,
A leaf, a fly, a spinning bubble—
  He did not see a troubled man.

For this, a moment in an age,
  He paid no price, and gave no thought ;
He ceased his spirit's weary search
  And took that instant all he sought.

FRANK KENDON

THE MAN IN THE BOWLER HAT

I am the unnoticed, the unnoticeable man :
The man who sat on your right in the morning train :
The man you looked through like a windowpane :
The man who was the colour of the carriage, the colour of
  the mounting
Morning pipe-smoke.

I am the man too busy with a living to live,
Too hurried and worried to see and smell and touch :
The man who is patient too long and obeys too much
And wishes too softly and seldom.

I am the man they call the nation's backbone,
Who am boneless—playable catgut, pliable clay :
The Man they label Little lest one day
I dare to grow.

I am the rails on which the moment passes,
The megaphone for many words and voices :
I am graph, diagram,
Composite face.

I am the led, the easily-fed,
The tool, the not-quite-fool,
The would-be-safe-and-sound,
The uncomplaining, bound,
The dust fine-ground,
Stone-for-a-statue waveworn pebble-round.

A. S. J. TESSIMOND

HOUND VOICE

Because we love bare hills and stunted trees
And were the last to choose the settled ground,
Its boredom of the desk or of the spade, because
So many years companioned by a hound,
Our voices carry ; and though slumber-bound,
Some few half wake and half renew their choice,
Give tongue, proclaim their hidden name—' Hound Voice.'

The women that I picked spoke sweet and low
And yet gave tongue. ' Hound Voices ' were they all.
We picked each other from afar and knew
What hour of terror comes to test the soul,
And in that terror's name obeyed the call,
And understood, what none have understood,
Those images that waken in the blood.

Some day we shall get up before the dawn
And find our ancient hounds before the door,
And wide awake know that the hunt is on ;
Stumbling upon the blood-dark track once more,
Then stumbling to the kill beside the shore ;
Then cleaning out and bandaging of wounds,
And chants of victory amid the encircling hounds.

W. B. YEATS

SPRING NIGHT

Spring night, the owls crying
From copse to copse and the dew rising.

Then wonderful the empty field and waiting
For another people to be returning
From the dark rain and the jealous forest
Into their rest.

Still be that pathless place of comfort
And fair the flowering they sought :
Even the long-eared grasses in compassion
Ceasing their talk of scythe and resurrection.

Wise be the woods, and every pale-throated
Primrose at peace, you undevoted :
Cunning the river as your subtle thoughts
Turning a stone to blue or black-eyed quartz.

Unmoved the leaf, light lie the soil about
The fierce endeavour of the root :
Come not with your unquiet voice
Bidding the solitude rejoice.

Never so quiet be eye and grief
Though bone its panacea receive
Blood calls to blood and humours wrap
The tortuous runway of the sap.

O leave us, you lover, cease telling
Of sorrow past our healing :
Sleep and cease crying, you wounded
Against the undefended.

Spring night, plovers calling
Over the fallow and the dew falling.

SIDNEY KEYES

THE BIRD

Adventurous bird walking upon the air,
Like a schoolboy running and loitering, leaping and springing,
Pensively pausing, suddenly changing your mind
To turn at ease on the heel of a wing-tip. Where
In all the crystalline world was there to find
For your so delicate walking and airy winging
A floor so perfect, so firm and so fair,
And where a ceiling and walls so sweetly ringing
Whenever you sing, to your clear singing?

The wide-winged soul itself can ask no more
Than such pure, resilient and endless floor
For its strong-pinioned plunging and soaring and upward
and upward springing.

EDWIN MUIR

THE FOX

First lambs have come, late snowfall to the hill.
All day he watches, feeding on greed
till, stars in the April sky, he steals
shadowy down the valleyside, furtive wades
marsh myrtle and by screen of heather comes
where flocks graze. Trembling for quarry
he scans each plucking lamb, chooses, pauses
strong as a spell, then flashes to revelry.

The lambless ewe sputters down the slope.
Home over Bristly Ridge in one sweep
he covers the Glyders, then deviously to his deep
mountain den, safe down creviced drop
where no terrier dares.

On his morning round
death in wool embers is the shepherd's find.

IAN SERRAILLIER

EPITHALAMION

Wind in the street, and sadness of unknown walkers
in a world shut-out ; infinite sadness of men
not, this night, one and quiet with my love :
look down, stars, you illimitable and glorious wakers,
on her delight that wakes from silks ; her, the young moon,
her bright body stepping to me, perfect, unaloof,
moving in life ;
rising with no shame, towards Endymion.

Oh swift lights that sweep through your proud abysses,
and stretch your power along the infinitesimal days of man,
this shall escape you, this you shall not dissolve.
Have we not checked you, winging wind, stars in your courses,
bound you in a twilight of all times, made our demesne
in the still courts of the chimera, silenced moment and self ?
together, the gulf
walled-in, body and life made one ?

Life in life, spirit in spirit, as the earth moves
for ever gently in the swaying of night's harness,
one peace ; as now earth rests, and all the
ships have untroubled ways in their white grooves,
and waters go among them on caressing journeys ;
and our imprisoned prophecy steals wide and free
as the pouring pools of the sea,
strong indissoluble wonder of deep clearness ?

No future, no fear now, in this hushed house stirring ;
only our breaths bound, linked the circle of our years,
and the past rising present against sleep.
I have taken the world in a small room, oh high staring
night, our flesh made perfect ; mine to be ours.
And the strong promise lays its head upon my lap :
him will I keep,
Here in the burning of our mutual fires.

And the fires burn down ; faces return from glass ;
we are not waking, dead, sleeping : we are still,
in timelessness, the flower shaken from the bough.
And shadows move in the deep breath of weariness ;
in peace, unknowing, endeavour turns to the wall.
And the wheel's quietness is promise. Now
we murmuring only know
the immemorial splendour of the wheel.

TERENCE TILLER

THE ATOLL IN THE MIND

Out of what calms and pools the cool shell grows
dumb teeth under clear waters, where no currents
fracture the coral's porous horn

Grows up the mind's stone tree, the honeycomb,
the plump brain coral breaking the pool's mirror,
the ebony antler, the cold sugared fan.

All these strange trees stand upward through the water,
the mind's grey candied points tend to the surface,
the greater part is out of sight below.

But when on the island's whaleback spring green blades,
new land over water wavers, birds bring seeds
and tides plant slender trunks by the lagoon

I find the image of the mind's two trees, cast downward,
one tilting leaves to catch the sun's bright pennies,
one dark as water rooted among the bones.

ALEX COMFORT

LACHRYMÆ

Slow are the years of light :
                                        and more immense
Than the imagination. And the years return
Until the Unity is filled. And heavy are
The lengths of Time with the slow weight of tears.
Since Thou didst weep, on a remote hillside
Beneath the olive trees, fires of unnumbered stars
Have burnt the years away, until we see them now :
Since Thou didst weep, as many tears
Have flowed like hourglass sand.
Thy tears were all.
And when our secret face
Is blind because of the mysterious
Surging of tears wrung by our most profound
Presentiment of evil in man's fate, our cruellest wounds
Become Thy stigmata. They are Thy tears which fall.

DAVID GASCOYNE

NOTHING IS ENOUGH

Nothing is enough !
No, though our all be spent—
Heart's extremest love,
Spirit's whole intent,
All that nerve can feel,
All that brain invent,—
Still beyond appeal
Will Divine Desire
Yet more excellent
Precious cost require
Of this mortal stuff,—
Never be content
Till ourselves be fire,
Nothing is enough !

LAURENCE BINYON

THE THREE STARS OF PROPHECY

The night was Time :
The phases of the moon,
Dynamic influence, controller of the tides,
The changing face and cycle of quick shades,
Were History, which seemed unending. Then
Occurred the prophesied and the to be
Recounted hour when the reflection ceased
To flow like unseen life-blood in between
The night's tenebral mirror and the lunar light,
Exchanging meaning. Anguish like a crack
Ran with its ruin from the fulfilled Past
Towards the Future's emptiness ; and *black*,
Invading all the prism, became absolute.

Black was the No-time at the heart
Of Time (the frameless mirror's back),
But still the Anguish shook
As though with memory and with anticipation : till
Its terror's trembling broke
By an unhoped-for miracle Negation's spell :
Death died and Birth was born with one great cry
And out of some uncharted spaceless sky
Into the new-born night three white stars fell.

And were suspended there a while for all
To see and understand (though none may tell
The inmost meaning of this Mystery).
The first star has a name which stands
For many names of all things that begin
And all first thoughts of undivided minds ;
The second star
Is nameless and shines bleakly like the pain
Of an existence conscious only of its end,
And inarticulate, alone
And blind. Immeasurably far
Each from the other first and second spin ;
Yet to us at this moment they appear

So close to one another that their rays
In one blurred conflagration intertwine;
So that the third seems born
Of their embracing: till the outer pair
Are separate seen again
Fixed in their true extremes; and in between
These two gleams' hemispheres, unseen
But shining everywhere,
The third star balanced shall henceforward burn
Through all dark still to come, serene,
Ubiquitous, immaculately clear;
A magnet in the middle of the maze, to draw us on
Towards that Bethlehem beyond despair
Where from the womb of Nothing shall be born
A Son.

DAVID GASCOYNE

HOC EST CORPUS

I who am nothing and this tissue
steer, find in my servant still my maker,
rule and obey, as flame to candle mated:
whom bone has conjured, Banquo shall the Bard
command, the marble rule Pygmalion.
Did this tower build me then who am its garrison?

Strange that in me the shadow
moving the substance speaks: strange that such air
pulls the blue sinew, whom the blood maintains,
whom the heart's coming slight defection
shall spill, speaks now and holds
time like a permanent stone, its cold weight judging.

ALEX COMFORT

PIETA

Stark in the pasture on the skull-shaped hill,
In swollen aura of disaster shrunken and
Unsheltered by the ruin of the sky,
Intensely concentrated in themselves the banded
Saints abandoned kneel.

And under the unburdened tree
Great in their midst, the rigid folds
Of a blue cloak upholding as a text
Her grief-scrawled face for the ensuing world to read,
The Mother, whose dead Son's dear head
Weighs like a precious blood-encrusted stone
On her unfathomable breast :
Holds Him God has forsaken, Word made flesh
Made ransom, to the slow smoulder of her heart
Till the catharsis of the race shall be complete.

DAVID GASCOYNE

POEM

The grecian tulip and the gothic rose
flower to deceive us ; limbs age with fruits ;
the man who marks the boneyard with a cross
reaps poppies ; human flesh plucks down the roots
of the barley. The greyhound with the kind
sensitive head and the soft eyes, goes blind
or mad ; dies. The wind means all it cries.
Love, it is time we listened to that wind.

Who cranes an arm to wait for the white body,
death, polishing old philosophies,
gives the grave scarves woven of our beauty.
Beasts are passive as growing rings of trees ;
perfected process lacking hope or thought,
tulip-limbs, or the white rose in the throat.
To die as those die, live as the lion knows
—love, it is time we found that secret out.

TERENCE TILLER

THE CRYSTAL

With burning fervour
I am forever
Turning in my hand
The crystal, this moment

Whose spatial glitter
Travelling erratically
Forward

Touches with permanent
Disturbance the pavements
The faked walls the crevices
Of futurity.

Sooner than darken
This crystal miracle
With a hand's
Vagary

One would dissever
This wrist this hand,
Or remove the eyelid
To see the end.

GEORGE BARKER

THE BURNING OF THE LEAVES

Now is the time for the burning of the leaves.
They go to the fire ; the nostril pricks with smoke
Wandering slowly into the weeping mist.
Brittle and blotched, ragged and rotten sheaves !
A flame seizes the smouldering ruin, and bites
On stubborn stalks that crackle as they resist.

The last hollyhock's fallen tower is dust :
All the spices of June are a bitter reek,
All the extravagant riches spent and mean.
All burns ! the reddest rose is a ghost.
Sparks whirl up, to expire in the mist : the wild
Fingers of fire are making corruption clean.

Now is the time for stripping the spirit bare,
Time for the burning of days ended and done,
Idle solace of things that have gone before.
Rootless hope and fruitless desire are there :
Let them go to the fire with never a look behind.
The world that was ours is a world that is ours no more.

They will come again, the leaf and the flower, to arise
From squalor of rottenness into the old splendour,
And magical scents to a wondering memory bring ;
The same glory, to shine upon different eyes.
Earth cares for her own ruins, naught for ours.
Nothing is certain, only the certain spring.

LAURENCE BINYON

INDEX OF TITLES AND FIRST LINES

[Titles are printed in *italics*]